THE
ULTIMATE GUIDE

TO VA LOANS

Grant Moon

This book is dedicated to the men and women who have sacrificed in defending our freedom and making the world a better place in which to live. Thank you to those currently serving and carrying on our proud history of defending our liberties, and to those who have done what so few Americans do today—to wear a uniform. Finally, a special thank you goes to my family and friends for the motivation and support.

TABLE OF CONTENTS

ABOUT THE AUTHOR

Grant Moon

Grant Moon is the founder and CEO of VALC Enterprises, the parent Company of Home Captain, Inc. He has 18 years of experience as an Enlisted Soldier and Commissioned Officer in the Army National Guard and Army Reserves. Grant has served in numerous capacities throughout his service, including Military Policeman, Rifle Platoon Leader, Rifle Company Executive Officer, Battalion Operations Officer, Battle Captain, Company Commander, and Joint Operations Center Executive Officer. Grant is a proud veteran of Operation Iraqi Freedom.

Throughout his service, Grant's has earned high esteems as a leader and his accolades include a Bronze Star Medal, Army Commendation Medal, and two Army Achievement Medals. He was the Distinguished Military Graduate of his Officer Candidate School Class, as well as the recipient of the Leadership Award from the Association of the United States Army. He currently serves as a Major in the United

States Army Reserves as the European Command Joint Operations Center Executive Officer.

Grant founded Home Captain in 2012 after identifying a need in the market to educate the community in using their benefits when buying a home and to get the best rates and fees. He went on to author *The Ultimate Guide to VA Loans*. Today, Home Captain provides real estate technology and brokerage services for a number of nationwide banks, Army Times, Air Force Times, Navy Times, Marine Times, Military Times, and Stars and Stripes. Finally, VA Loan Captain holds a government contract in helping service members leverage their benefits regarding home ownership.

Prior to founding Home Captain, Grant had extensive experience in leading real estate, e-commerce, sales, marketing, and distribution departments within publicly traded companies.

Grant has an MS in Technology Management from Columbia University, an MBA from Babson College, and a BS from Endicott College.

INTRODUCTION

This is the second edition of my first book, *The Ultimate Guide to VA Loans*, which was first published and released in 2013. As the entire mortgage industry has taken its fair share of twists and turns, the VA mortgage program has also adapted over time. The purpose of this edition is to update new VA guidelines and introduce this special program once again to those who have served in the military.

This book is written by a veteran who has taken advantage of his VA entitlement and used it to buy real estate. While containing the breadth of information needed to understand how VA loans work, this book is more like a compilation of many books merged into one.

The following chapters could well be individual books in their own right. You can turn to any of these and get a complete understanding of the topics covered, without having to review previous chapters or have information explained to you in later chapters.

There are different property types to which VA loans can be applied. There's a chapter dedicated to VA loan uses. Additionally, there is a chapter explaining the tax advantages of a VA loan. Another chapter delves into credit and credit scores. There's even a section on how you can use a VA loan in conjunction with building a home from the ground up. Did you know there's also a "jumbo" VA loan? All in all, this compilation consists of 20 distinct books into one.

As you review the titles of each chapter, you can turn immediately to the topic that interests you most for your specific situation. You can also treat this as any other book and start from the beginning, reading it in its entirety. There's also a glossary of loan terms at the end of the book for your use – you'll find it handy as you begin shopping for your new home or when you are considering the refinancing of your current VA mortgage loan.

VA loans have increased in popularity over the years and has always been the best performing loan program when compared to FHA and USDA loans and even conventional mortgage loans underwritten to Fannie Mae or Freddie Mac guidelines. The VA home loan is a benefit; it is an entitlement issued to veterans and other qualified service members in exchange for their courageous duty of service.

1

WHAT IS A VA LOAN?

The VA loan is a home mortgage loan that is underwritten and approved under lending guidelines established by the Department of Veterans Affairs (VA). It is one of the most popular VA benefits in existence today. One reason for the VA home loan's popularity is that it requires no down payment. Another reason is that credit and qualifying guidelines are more relaxed when compared to conventional mortgage programs.

What is the history of the VA loan program? In 1944, Congress passed the Servicemen's Readjustment Act – a legislation that provided a wide breadth of benefits to our returning troops from World War II. This act was established to help reinstate our troops back into civilian life with benefits such as business loans, as well as farm and home loan guarantees.

The Servicemen's Readjustment Act is more widely known as the G.I. Bill, which remains the term used to identify this package of benefits to this day. However, the VA mortgage loan program was only developed over the past few decades to improve and expand the program.

Congress authorized the VA to guarantee these types of loan types, should they default. When a bank makes a VA loan, the original lender making the VA loan would be reimbursed by approximately 20 percent of the original loan amount should the loan go into foreclosure, provided the lender approved the loan under VA lending guidelines and there was no indication of fraud. Notice that we mentioned it was "a bank" that approved a VA loan. It is noteworthy that the VA does not get involved in any direct way with approving or processing a VA home loan application; instead, approved VA lenders do, such as banks.

Initially, this special VA program was available only to those who returned from World War II. It had established certain cut-off or termination dates which veterans had to respect if they were to take advantage of the VA loan. This was especially attractive during that time, as many home loans from banks required 30, 40 and even 50% down payment.

Since then, the VA loan program has grown significantly and is now a staple of the mortgage industry. Initially, the VA home loan benefit was considered a temporary program to help returning veterans buy a home and establish credit. It was intended to be used only once, provided the veteran applied for their VA loan before their cutoff date. These cutoff dates were strict and required veterans to apply for a VA home loan within two years after their discharge or two years after the end of World War II.

However, because they were unaware of such cut-off dates or the program itself, many veterans were unable to take advantage of the VA mortgage program. In 1952, Congress extended the VA home loan benefits to veterans of the Korean War, as well as the cut-off date to 10 years after the end of the war or after an honorable discharge.

In 1960, Congress discovered that regardless of the additional cutoff dates, the VA home loan was still issued fewer times than in the previous 15 years. There was still work to be done to support veterans return to civilian life.

Congress found itself constantly providing legislation to accommodate veterans of both World War II and Korea and their new realities upon their return. Finally, in 1970, Congress passed the Veterans Housing Act that eliminated cut-off dates in the application of qualifying veterans for the VA home loan program as well as a host of other benefits in what is now known as the VA Home Loan Benefit.

Still, later in 1992, Congress again amended the original G.I. Bill by passing the Veterans Home Loan Program Amendments of 1992. This change expanded the VA home loan program to allow those other than world war veterans to apply, including those who served in the United States Army Reserve, Marine Forces Reserve, United Sates Navy Reserve, the Air Force Reserve Command and the United States Coast Guard. The United States National Guard, which includes the Army National Guard and the Air National Guard, can also benefit from the VA Home Loan.

It is still widely believed that the VA mortgage loan program is eligible only to veterans. However, there are so many more individuals who can avail of this benefit. Who are these groups specifically? The Department of Veterans Affairs divides those eligible into three separate categories, identified as Group A, B and C.

Group A includes veterans, those serving on Active Duty and Armed Forces Reservists, as well as National Guard Members who have served on active duty.

These veterans must have served in World War II, the Korean War or Vietnam War. They must be honorably discharged or have served during peacetime with a minimum of 181 days of active duty. As for Armed Forces Reserves and National Guard Members who have served on active duty for Active Duty personnel, they must be on regular duty after continuous service of 181 days.

Group B includes other Armed Forces Reserves and National Guard members who have not served on Active Duty, but who have served for at least six years and were honorably discharged.

Group C is reserved for the surviving spouses of veterans who died while serving or due to a service-connected disability.

There is a final category specifically for selected members of other government agencies, which includes those in service as Public Health Service Officers, cadets at the United States Military Academy, Air Force Academy, Coast Guard Academy, midshipmen at the Naval Academy, officers at the National Oceanic and Atmospheric Administration and certain merchant seamen who served during World War II.

That's quite a list. Indeed, the VA home loan program is open to many others, although these individuals are often unaware of their eligibility.

How does the program work, and how can the VA guarantee a mortgage when conventional loans carry no such guarantee?

A borrower will first determine if he or she is eligible for the program. This is achieved by obtaining the Certificate of Eligibility (COE) from the Department of Veterans Affairs, which will be discussed further in detail in Chapter 2.

After obtaining the COE, the borrower contacts a lender who is approved to underwrite VA home loans. The borrower then gets prequalified for a loan amount and finds a home to buy that is within their budget.

A borrower is not required to make a down payment on a VA home loan. While making a down payment is not prohibited under the program, rarely does a borrower provide one on a VA home loan. A detailed comparison on various loan types will be considered in Chapter 3.

The VA guarantee is primarily funded by what is called the VA Funding Fee, which is in essence an insurance policy for which the veteran pays that helps fund the guarantee program. If a VA home loan goes into default, the original lender may be eligible for a refund which amounts to approximately 25% of the defaulted loan. The only veteran borrowers exempt from the VA Funding Fee are those who have incurred a service-related disability.

Historically, those who take a VA home loan have the best loan performance pricing when compared to all other loan types, including mortgages underwritten to Fannie Mae and Freddie Mac (conventional) loans and FHA mortgage loans, which all require some sort of down payment. The notion that home buyers who don't have "skin in the game" in terms of a down payment and a mortgage are more likely to default is simply false.

The funding fee can change based on a variety of factors including the type of service, down payment amount, a refinance and subsequent use of a VA home loan. It is expressed as a percentage of the loan amount and may be paid in cash; however, it is most always included into the loan amount and may be borrowed as part of the mortgage and paid out over the term of the loan.

For example, a first-time veteran borrower will find a 2.15% funding fee that is required for the loan. On a $200,000 loan, the funding fee is $4,300, with the final loan amount totaling $204,300. Costs and fees will be discussed in greater detail in Chapter 4.

The VA Home Loan has risen in popularity over the years, primarily due to the efforts of the Department of Veteran Affairs to educate lenders and individual mortgage loan officers on the program.

The Popularity of VA Loans

As previously stated, the primary and obvious reason for the program's popularity is that it does not require a down payment. It remains the biggest advantage for veterans, but there are others.

A borrower with a VA home loan can have up to 41% or more of their gross monthly income dedicated to a housing payment, while a conventional mortgage has its standard housing income guideline at 28%.

Over the past two decades, there have been several attempts at introducing different mortgage programs to the market that required little or no money down and had reduced credit standards. These programs grew in popularity in the 2000's but soon fell out of favor with both the public and regulatory agencies as their delinquency rates soared and were thus considered by many to be one of the main contributors to the housing crisis.

VA credit requirements are relaxed when compared to conventional fare. While the VA does not directly issue a minimum credit score requirement, most VA lenders do establish a minimum credit score of 620 from its borrowers. Furthermore, conventional loans that accept that same credit score typically require a down payment of 10 percent or more on the sales price of the home. For example, on a $200,000 loan with a 620 credit score, a conventional loan might require a down payment of $20,000! Interestingly, even with credit scores below 620, VA-qualified borrowers may still obtain a VA mortgage with certain lenders who can approve a loan by implementing a "manual" underwriting method that does not require a minimum score.

Another significant advantage of a VA home loan is the reduced closing costs that a borrower may pay. The VA has placed restrictions on the closing costs that can be charged to a veteran. Such closing costs must be paid by the lender or the seller of the property.

These advantages have contributed to more than 20 million home loans that have received the VA guarantee since the VA mortgage program's inception. Recent figures show that there were more than 740,000 VA loans issued in 2017 alone, resulting in the highest level of loan activity in more than 25 years.

Uses

A VA home loan can be used for a variety of purposes, the first being the purchase of a home. A VA purchase money mortgage can be used to buy a single-family residence, a duplex, a 3-4 unit (triplex or fourplex), a condominium, a coop, and manufactured and mobile housing. One of the main requirements for purchase of any of these properties is that it must be owner-occupied and not used as an investment property.

However, a VA home loan can also be used for a refinance loan regardless if the original loan was a VA loan or not. A VA refinance mortgage can be a VA to VA refinance, a Federal Housing Administration (FHA) to VA refinance or a conventional to VA refinance loan. Why would someone refinance into a VA loan when the existing mortgage is not a VA loan? A VA loan can be refinanced up to 100% of its value while other loan programs require up to 10 percent in equity before a refinance is possible.

During a refinance, sometimes qualified borrowers may decide to pull out additional equity in the form of cash. There are three types of VA mortgages refinancing: a rate and term refinance; a streamlined or Interest Rate Reduction Refinance Loan (IRRRL); and an IRRRL and a cash out refinance.

There are also allowances for construction loans, although it may be difficult, if not impossible, to find a lender who issues a VA construction mortgage. Rather than obtain a VA Construction Loan, you can opt for a traditional construction loan from a bank and use your VA eligibility to pay it off with a VA loan.

You may also take advantage of a VA Home Improvement Loan which provides a guarantee for funds used to make existing homes more energy efficient. It offers funds of up to $6,000 for items such as heating and air conditioning systems, storm windows, insulation and other green improvements.

Summary

- The VA Home Loan was originally authorized by Congress in 1944 to help compensate returning World War II veterans and help readjust the troops back into civilian life.

- Initially, the VA Home Loan was not as successful with its intended beneficiaries, primarily due to strict cutoff or termination dates veterans had to observe or they would otherwise lose the benefit.

- VA loans served very few veterans in the 15 years prior to 1961, despite the number of returning troops from the Korean War amounting to the thousands.

- The VA does not provide a VA loan; rather, it establishes lending guidelines for lenders to follow. The VA guarantees a portion of the original VA mortgage should the loan ever go into default, provided that the lender followed the VA lending rules. Lenders make the loan; VA guarantees them.

- The VA loan's performance has the lowest delinquency rate of any mortgage program.

- The 1970 Veterans Housing Act modernized the VA Home Loan Benefit, eliminating cutoff dates, thus expanding the benefit to a wider pool of service members and establishing new programs.

- There have been more than 20 million VA guaranteed mortgage loans issued since the program's inception.

- The VA guarantee is funded by the Funding Fee, which refers to a percentage of the loan amount paid by the borrower and typically rolled into the loan amount.

- The VA Home Loan consists of no money down, easier qualifying and relaxed credit guidelines.

- The VA home loan can be used for a variety of property types; however, it must always be issued for a primary residence and is not eligible for an investment property.

2

VA LOAN USES

In the previous chapter, we discussed general uses for a VA home loan based on property type. This chapter will discuss these eligible property types in more detail.

What types of property are eligible for a VA home loan guarantee? These include:

- Single-family

- Multi-family

- Condominium homes

- Cooperatives

- Manufactured homes

- Mobile homes and land

- Construction

- Energy efficiency improvements

The most common property type financed with a VA home loan is the single-family home. This type of home has its own lot and is not attached to any other unit. Often, this type of home is described as "single family-detached" to indicate that the exterior walls are not physically adjacent to any other property and occupied; moreover, it rest on land upon which is owned by the property owner.

Multi-Family

For the purposes of VA mortgages, a multi-family home refers to any residential structure that shares one or more walls up to four units. The most common multi-family structure is the duplex, where two separate dwellings are attached by a common wall. The VA loan requires that the qualified VA borrower live in one of the two units.

The next most common type of multi-family structure is called a "2-4 building," which refers to a property with two, three or four separate dwellings sharing exterior walls. All units must have their own entryways and one of the units must be occupied by the qualified VA borrower.

Condominium Homes

A condominium home (or "condo") is a type of property where the owner of the condo owns the interior structure of the dwelling, as well as all permanent appliances and improvements within the unit. Areas surrounding the individual unit externally are owned by all condo owners jointly and equally; they are called "common areas," which include public spaces such as sidewalks, swimming pools, parks, recreation rooms. Moreover, heating and cooling equipment may also be shared amongst condo owners.

Condos are typically characterized by multiple units sharing walls, and its physical appearance resembles any standard apartment building. While most condominium projects consist of attached units, there are others that comprise a series of duplexes, 2-4 units and even single-family structures. The definition of a condominium lies in the legal structure and ownership of the project.

A condominium is governed by "conditions" – covenants and restrictions that all owners must agree to and abide by. Such restrictions might include any exterior work or design, such as the inclusion of patios or front doors. The condo is typically managed by a homeowners' association which helps to enforce condominium rules among its other tasks.

A condominium must be approved by the VA to be eligible for VA financing. The Department of Veterans Affairs keeps a list of approved condominium projects on its website, which can also be delivered by fax or mail. A VA lender will inform the borrower if a condominium is VA-approved.

For a condominium project to obtain VA approval, it must meet specific requirements. For instance, the project cannot be involved in any litigation. The VA also requires more than 50 percent of the units to be owner- occupied, not rented. Furthermore, the condominium's legal documentation must be reviewed prior to VA approval.

Cooperatives

A cooperative (or "coop") refers to a legal entity, such as a partnership, corporation or limited liability corporation (LLC), that owns real estate. A coop's appearance is similar to an apartment building or attached condos.

An owner of a dwelling in a coop owns a legal share of the coop, which gives them the right to occupy one or more of the units depending on how many shares the owner bought. Buyers are usually screened by a coop committee that can approve or deny their application for a share (dwelling). Like a condominium association, the coop's shareholders must agree to specific rules enforced by their elected governing body.

Manufactured Homes

Manufactured homes are structures built by prefabricated pieces and assembled at a manufacturing facility. They are then transported to a dealer or directly to the buyer or owner's property.

A manufactured home is strictly defined as being completed at a factory. Therefore, this definition applies to mobile homes as well, as they are built in a factory then delivered to its site, where it will be fixed permanently to the land.

However, a manufactured home can also be considered a "modular home" and the terms are sometimes confused. A modular home is built with prefabricated components which are subsequently delivered to the construction site. Whereas a mobile home is completed at a factor, a modular home is only completed at its final destination.

Mobile Homes and Land

This type of property is a combination of both the mobile home and the land upon which it sits. A similar comparison for this type of real estate is a single-family home in which a loan is made for both the structure as well as the land.

Mobile homes may be purchased separately as can raw land, but this transaction includes both simultaneously.

Construction

A construction loan is used to build a property from the ground up. It provides funds for both "hard" and "soft" costs. A "hard" cost refers to a cost for labor and materials, while a "soft" cost is reserved for permits and plans.

A construction loan is a temporary loan, only until completion of the property's construction. At the end of the construction period, the construction loan must be replaced by a permanent mortgage.

The VA will guarantee a construction loan; however, that does not mean a lender will issue VA construction loan.

Energy Efficient Improvements

The VA also issues guarantees for loans to homeowners that are used to improve the home's energy efficiency. This loan program can be used as a refinance or a purchase and it can include the costs of the energy improvements with specific dollar limitations.

These limitations consist of an extra $3,000 for energy improvements which are documented by invoices and paid receipts for items such as energy efficient windows, insulation and HVAC improvements. Another limit is set at $6,000 if the improvements will reduce energy costs.

Similarly, with VA construction loans, while the VA may provide a guarantee for an energy efficient mortgage, lenders are not obliged to offer them.

Pros and Cons

This section describes the various advantages and disadvantages for the different property types and uses for a VA home loan. Many are based on personal preferences but also on the availability of the specific loan from VA lenders.

Single-Family

Pros: The single-family VA loan is the most widely used VA home loan product which results in lower, more competitive interest rates and more lenders offering the programs. There are more single-family homes for sale than any other residential property, thus providing more choices in home styles, sizes, price and locations.

Cons: Single-family homes require maintenance and upkeep, along with property taxes and homeowner's insurance, which may not be required with other types of property.

Multi-Family Homes

Pros: Living in a multi-family home provides the opportunity to offset the total costs of home ownership, including mortgage interest, taxes, insurance and fees.

Cons: There aren't as many multi-family homes for sale, and lenders can increase the interest rates and down payment requirements for such loans. Moreover, living next to tenants provides less privacy for the owners, who also become landlords responsible for the maintenance and repair of their tenants' unit.

Condominium Home

Pros: This property type offers typically lower cost per square foot compared to single-family homes in similar neighborhoods. A condo requires much less maintenance, as common areas are maintained by the condominium management that is financed by homeowners' association fees.

Cons: Conditions, covenants and restrictions can sometimes prove to be a burden to homeowners. Rules are enforced by management and a homeowners' association. There is relatively little ability to personalize the exterior of one's condominium home. The condominium project must also be approved by the VA prior to the issue of any VA loan by a VA lender.

Cooperatives

Pros: Coops have lower costs for ownership and require less maintenance compared to condominium homes and apartments.

Cons: Most coops are in densely populated areas and are not widely available. Few lenders issue VA loans for coops.

Manufactured Homes

Pros: Manufactured homes are much less expensive compared to single-family, multi-family and condominium properties.

Cons: Interest rates tend to be higher for manufactured homes. Furthermore, not all VA lenders provide financing for manufactured housing.

Construction

Pros: VA construction loans allow the borrower to build their own home with their own architectural plans rather than buying an existing home or one built by a developer.

Cons: Although there is a VA guarantee for a construction loan, finding a lender to issue a VA construction loan is difficult at best.

Energy Efficient Improvements

Pros: It is an inexpensive and convenient process to improve a home's energy efficiency through thermal windows, caulking, up-to-date thermostats and other green improvements.

Cons: Few—if any—lenders issue a VA energy efficiency mortgage regardless of the VA guarantee and guidelines.

Summary

- The VA home loan guarantee program is open to nearly any type of residential property.
- The VA provides special underwriting requirements for different property types.
- All property types must be owner-occupied.
- Regardless of any VA guarantee, it is up to the individual lender to participate in the VA loan program.

3

VA LOAN TYPES

This chapter will discuss and review in detail the various loan types offered by VA lenders and that are guaranteed by the Department of Veterans Affairs. This chapter will also help identify which loan type best meets your requirements.

In order to determine which VA loan is best for you, you'll need to consider the amortization, or length of the loan, and whether the rate is fixed or can adjust periodically throughout the loan term.

Loan types can also be in the form of a purchase mortgage or refinance loan.

VA loan types are also characterized by their loan amounts. Lenders can issue VA mortgage loans with limits for standard or conforming VA loan limits, and for higher loan limits in the form of VA Jumbo Loans. The VA loan types are:

- 30-year fixed
- 15-year fixed
- Fixed rate options
- 5/1 Hybrid
- 3/1 Hybrid
- VA Jumbo

- VA Streamline Refinance (IRRRL)
- VA Cash-Out Refinance

30-Year Fixed

All fixed rates have one thing in common: their interest rate never changes. Therefore, the monthly mortgage payment never changes. The only thing that changes within a fixed rate mortgage is the amount devoted to the principal and to the interest of each payment.

All VA mortgage loans are fully amortized, meaning the loan is completely paid off at a predetermined point in the future. Each monthly payment is divided and put toward principal and interest in disparate amounts. At the beginning of each loan, most of the monthly payment goes toward interest, whereas very little will go towards principal. As the end of the loan term approaches, more and more is applied to the principal balance and less toward interest.

This disparity is due to the calculation of the interest on a fully amortized loan. The interest rate is based on the current, outstanding principal balance each month. At the beginning of the loan term, the principal balance is much larger – hence, the higher interest calculation. As the loan progressively gets paid off, the outstanding principal balance is reduced, resulting in a lesser amount going towards interest.

The 30-year fixed rate mortgage offers the lowest monthly payment compared to other fixed rate terms.

15-Year Fixed

The second most popular fixed rate VA mortgage is the 15-year fixed rate loan. Like the 30-year fixed rate VA loan, the interest rate also never changes, nor do the monthly principal and interest payment. Thus, because the loan is both fixed and fully amortized, the loan will be paid off in exactly 15 years or in 180 equal installments.

In addition, each payment has more interest paid during the early years of the mortgage and less towards the end of the loan. The rate on a 15-year fixed VA mortgage will be slightly lower compared to a 30-year loan term, typically by one-eighth to one-quarter percent.

Fixed Rate Options

Many VA lenders also provide other options regarding fixed rate loan terms. These optional terms are in five- year increments including 15-, 20-, 25 and 30-year fixed rate loan programs. The rate never changes, and the monthly principal and interest payment remain the same throughout the loan term.

As with all fixed rate and fully amortized loans, there is more interest is for the VA lender towards the beginning of the loan and less toward the end of the loan term.

Many VA borrowers—in fact, many mortgage borrowers in general—are often only quoted 15- and 30-year fixed rate loan programs, unaware there are other options available. Many times, the loan officer may not be aware of such an offering. However, it remains something important to consider. Why?

The difference in monthly payment between a 30-year fixed rate loan and a 15-year fixed rate loan can be surprising to most people. Although the interest rate on a 15-year fixed rate loan is lower than a 30-year fixed rate, the monthly payment is higher because the loan must be paid off twice as fast.

As an example, consider the difference between a 15- and 30-year $200,000 VA mortgage loan:

Fixed Rate Option	Interest Rate	Monthly Payment
30-year	4.00%	$954.83
15-year	3.75%	$1,454.44

That's a difference of $499.61 every month.

Consider now the difference in interest paid over the span of that same loan:

30-year fixed rate payment at 4.00% interest paid = $143,738

15-year fixed rate payment at 3.75% percent interest paid = $61,800

Fixed Rate Payment	Interest Paid	Monthly Payment
30-year	4.00%	$143,738
15-year	3.75%	$61,800

Note: These rates are for illustration purposes only.

The difference in interest paid to the bank—and out of your pocket—is $81,938 over the span of the loan. It is for this reason borrowers tend apply for a 15-year fixed rate VA mortgage. However, because the monthly payments are higher, qualifying for the 15-year fixed rate loan can be more difficult.

Still, there are other choices – the 20- and 25-year fixed rate VA mortgage. Below is a table listing the differences in payment and interest for all four choices, using the same rate and loan amount from the previous examples.

Term	Rate	Payment	Interest
30-year	4.00%	$954.83	$143,739
25-year	4.00%	$1,055.67	$116,702
20-year	3.75%	$1,185.78	$84,586
15-year	3.75%	$1454.44	$61,800

As you can see, as the term shortens, the monthly payment rises. However, the amount of interest paid over the course of the loan is greater the longer the term and less for shorter terms.

If you would like a combination of a lower monthly payment than what is required in a 15-year fixed rate loan, yet you wish to save on interest, you may avail of the other options besides the popular 15- and 30-year fixed rate VA mortgage.

5/1 Hybrid

A 5/1 hybrid loan is fixed for five years then turns into an annual adjustable rate mortgage (or "ARM").

Although a hybrid loan could be thought of as a combination of a fixed rate mortgage and an ARM, for all intents and purposes it should be considered an adjustable rate mortgage.

The first digit in the 5/1 hybrid loan indicates the number of years in which the interest rate is fixed at the beginning of the loan. In this loan, the rate is fixed for 5 years. The second digit in this example, 1, indicates when the ARM adjusts after the initial 5 years. In the VA 5/1 hybrid ARM, it adjusts once per year.

The 5/1 hybrid also contains inherent borrower protections in the form of interest rate limits known as "caps," which limit how much an interest rate can change year over the year, as well as how high the interest rate can reach.

A "1% annual cap" means that the rate cannot go any higher than 1% over the previous rate. The lifetime cap on the VA 5/1 hybrid ARM is 5%, meaning the adjusted interest rate may never be higher than 5% over the initial rate.

As with all ARMs, once the hybrid reaches beyond the initial five-year period and begins to adjust, the new rate is calculated by adding a margin to an index. The index number is variable, but the VA 5/1 hybrid ARM is based on the one-year constant maturity index (or "CMT"). The VA margin can be 2.00 or 2.25%, depending on the VA lender's requirement.

At the end of one year, the margin is added to the one-year CMT to calculate the following year's interest rate. For example, if today's one-year CMT were 1.00% and the margin was 2.00%, the new rate would adjust to 1+2 = 3.00% for the next year.

Suppose the CMT rose to 5.00% in one year. Although it is unlikely, it is still possible. By adding the 2.00% margin to the 5.00% one-year CMT, the new rate would be 2+5= 7.00%! If the initial rate was 2.75% and after the first five years, the new rate increased to 7.00%, the rate would note adjust to 7.00% but to 3.75% due to the annual cap of 1 percent.

Furthermore, should the CMT index continue to rise to 9.00% in this example, due to the lifetime cap of 5.00 percent, the interest rate would never fully adjust to 11.00%; instead, it would stop at 7.75%.

3/1 Hybrid

The VA 3/1 hybrid is like the 5/1 VA hybrid, yet the initial fixed period is 3 years and not 5. Again, the second digit in the name of the loan, 1, indicates how often the rate will adjust after the initial 3-year period. This hybrid will adjust once per year.

The 3/1 VA hybrid is identical to the 5/1 VA hybrid in all aspects except for the initial fixed period. The index, margin and caps remain identical.

VA Jumbo

While the VA does not set specific loan limits (only VA lenders do), VA does limit the guarantee on a VA loan. In 39 states, the loan limit is $453,100 and the VA guarantee is 25% of that amount, or $113,275. In areas considered "high cost," VA loan limits may be as high as $679,650 or even more, depending upon the locale.

Still, lenders may still issue VA mortgages above the maximum loan limit. These VA mortgage loans are called VA Jumbo mortgages; however, like other VA mortgage products, not all lenders choose to offer them.

For example, a buyer finds a house that is listed at $650,000 and wants to use his VA loan entitlement to assist in the purchase. The VA will guarantee 25 percent of the lender's loan amount, which is $453,100 with no money down. Beyond that, the VA borrower will put down 25% of the difference between the sales price and the maximum $453,100.

In this instance, $650,000 - $453,100 = $196,900. 25% percent of that difference is $49,225, which represents the down payment amount the veteran is required to pay. This amounts to just less than 10% down for a jumbo mortgage which is very competitive in today's market.

The formula works for any VA jumbo mortgage, regardless of the sales price and maximum county loan limits in standard or high cost areas.

But where does the VA get these loan limits, and how are they set?

VA loan limits match conforming loan limits, i.e. conventional conforming loans underwritten to guidelines set by Fannie Mae and Freddie Mac.

The Federal Housing Finance Agency was established in 2008 as part of the original Federal Housing Finance Regulatory Reform Act of 2008. Prior to this legislation, there was no bona fide method in which Fannie Mae or Freddie Mac could follow when establishing loan limits.

At present, the Agency compares the national median home values from October to the values from October in the previous year. If there is a year-over-year increase, conforming loan limits will be adjusted accordingly for the following year. If there is a decrease, there will be no change. As the conforming loan limits change, so do the VA jumbo minimum loan amount.

There are three different types of loan limits set. The first and most common type consist of those that match conforming limits. The second is high balance in areas where home values are much higher compared to the rest of the country, and finally, the third type is jumbo. Conforming loans will have the lowest rate of the three, followed by high balance and jumbo, respectively.

VA Streamline Refinance (IRRRL)

The VA streamline refinance is different compared to a VA mortgage used to buy a property. Instead, it is used to change the rate or term of an existing VA home loan. The acronym "IRRRL" stands for "Interest Rate Reduction Refinance Loan" – it is most often simply called a "streamline" due to its simplicity and reduced documentation that is required to close the loan.

The streamline refinance loan stipulates that the existing loan that is being refinanced is considered a VA mortgage, sometimes referred to as a "VA to VA refinance". Reduced documentation of the VA streamline means no verification of employment or income information is completed, nor are any verification of assets or appraisal required. This reduced documentation and verification requirements dramatically reduce the time it takes to close the loan.

Although there is less documentation and no credit is reviewed, there are still some necessary requirements to qualify for the streamline refinance. The first requirement is a reduction in monthly payment due to the refinance. There is no guideline regarding how much lower the new payment must be compared to the current payment. This is no longer a requirement if the loan is going from an ARM to a fixed rate. Moreover, the borrower must also show evidence that they used their VA eligibility on the first loan as well. Credit scores or credit report reviews are not required. However, if there is evidence within the most recent 12-month period that a mortgage payment has not been made more than 30 days past the due date, this must be verified. Finally, while the borrower can roll closing costs into the loan amount, they cannot take out any equity in the form of cash at closing.

VA Cash-Out Refinance

A VA Cash-Out Refinance is like a standard refinance where only the rate and/or term is adjusted, with the difference being that cash is pulled out of the property at closing from equity into the property. Unlike the streamline refinance loan, the cash-out refinance is a fully documented loan requiring a complete qualification in terms of employment, credit and property valuations.

The VA guidelines for a cash-out refinance require that the loan amount not exceed 90% of the current appraised value of the property. For example, if the property is appraised at $300,000, then the maximum loan amount for a VA cash-out would be 90% of $300,000, or the amount of $270,000.

Using that same example, if the current loan payoff is $250,000 and closing costs are $5,000 for a total of $255,000, then at least the borrower would receive $15,000 cash proceeds from the difference of $270,000 to use for any purpose.

Unlike the VA streamline refinance, the existing mortgage does not have to be a VA loan – it can be any type of government or conventional mortgage.

It is important to highlight that while the VA may not require certain documentation or verification with a VA loan, that does not preclude a VA lender from imposing their own guidelines. For example, although the VA streamline loan program does not require an appraisal, a lender may still require one to fulfill their own internal compliance procedures.

4

VA LOAN FEES AND COSTS

VA loans, as with any mortgage loan on the market, are subject to closing costs to close the loan. These costs can originate with the VA lender and with third-party service providers, such as appraisers, credit reporting agencies and the VA itself.

The VA is very specific on the types of fees that may be charged to the VA borrower, and lenders must follow these specific guidelines to approve and fund a VA mortgage request properly.

The Funding Fee

The VA funding fee is the fee that VA charges to help subsidize the VA home loan program. It represents a percentage of the loan amount and may be rolled into the loan. Alternatively, it may be paid out-of-pocket by the veteran; however, nearly every VA loan has the funding fee already rolled into the mortgage.

The funding fee can be viewed as an insurance premium that the borrower pays to the benefit of the lender. When a VA loan goes into default and the home is foreclosed by the lender, the VA lender is guaranteed up to 25% of the outstanding loan amount, provided the lender employed proper VA underwriting techniques throughout the approval process and there is no evidence of fraud. It is the funding fee that helps offset the costs associated with a defaulted, guaranteed VA mortgage.

The funding fee is included on all VA mortgage loans with the exception of loans issued to veterans or service members who have a service-related disability. Veteran borrowers receiving disability pay from the VA are entitled to a waived funding fee.

The funding fee will also vary depending on the borrower's status, the number of times the borrower uses a VA loan, the existence of a down payment and the nature of the loan. The chart below will highlight the various funding fee requirements.

Funding Fee Amounts for First-Time Homebuyer

Down Payment %	Active Duty/Veteran	National Guard/Reserves
0	2.15%	2.40%
5-10	1.50%	1.75%
10+	1.25%	1.50%

Funding Fee Amounts for Subsequent Use

Down Payment %	Active Duty/Veteran	National Guard/Reserves
0	3.30%	3.30%
5-10	1.50%	1.75%
10+	1.25%	1.50%

Funding Fee Amounts for Cash-Out Refinance

Use	Active Duty/Veteran	National Guard/Reserves
First-Time	2.15%	2.40%
Subsequent Use	3.30%	3.30%

Funding Fee Amounts for Streamline Refinance (IRRRL)

Use	Active Duty/Veteran	National Guard/Reserves
First-Time	0.5%	0.5%
Subsequent Use	0.5%	0.5%

For example, a first-time homebuyer who is in active duty will see a funding fee of 2.15%. On a $200,000 VA loan, that would represent an additional $4,300 added to the loan, for a total of $204,300. If a qualifying National Guard member is applying for a VA cash-out refinance loan on a previous VA loan, the funding fee is 3.30%, or $6,600 on a $200,000 loan, for a total loan amount of $206,600.

Qualified VA borrowers benefit from the funding fee as it helps to finance the zero money down VA program when loan guarantees must be paid to VA lenders.

The funding fee is the only fee charged by and collected by the VA. There are no other required VA fees.

Closing Costs

Closing costs are an inherent feature of mortgages, including VA mortgages. Closing costs are typically divided into two categories: recurring and non-recurring. Recurring charges are fees that will be incurred repeatedly throughout the life of the mortgage loan, otherwise known as "prepaid charges" in the lending world. Non-recurring charges are fees that will occur one time and collected when the loan officially closes at the closing table. Non-recurring charges can refer to appraisals, credit reports and title insurance fees, among others.

Another benefit associated with a VA mortgage is the limits on the closing costs a VA borrower may pay. The VA has long established such a policy to protect the VA borrower from onerous charges instigated by third parties.

The VA has established that the VA borrower may only pay specific fees to third parties. An easy way to remember the charges a VA borrower may pay is the acronym, ACTORS.

- **A**ppraisal

- **C**redit Report

- **T**itle Insurance and Title Examination Fees

- **O**rigination Fees

- **R**ecording Charges

- **S**urvey or Abstract

Any other third-party fees are considered "non-allowable" and may not be charged to the veteran. Recurring charges, such as homeowners' insurance and interest charges, do not fall into that category.

A VA borrower may not pay any other fee directly, such as a loan processing fee, escrow or closing fees, or underwriting charges. However, these fees will typically exist on nearly all home loans and must be paid by the providers.

There are different scenarios that determine who will pay the veterans' non-allowable closing costs.

The first is during a purchase contract negotiation, wherein the VA borrower asks the seller to pay the restricted closing costs. Alternatively, a lender may agree to pay or otherwise waive the restricted charges, either as an adjustment in interest rate or through fee negotiations with the loan officer or lender.

Note, however, that it is not a requirement for the property seller to pay the restricted fees, nor is it a requirement imposed by a VA lender. Nevertheless, the fees still remain and must be paid before the loan can close. Historically, this situation could cause an impasse between a buyer and a seller; often, a seller will decline an offer that is being financed by a VA loan as soon as they become aware of the restricted fees.

In their recognition of this, the VA made recent adjustments to the restricted fee program where the lender could charge an origination fee of no greater than 1% of the loan amount rather than have the seller, lender or borrower pay the fees directly.

This change meant that a lender who typically charges a $500 underwriting fee and a $500 processing fee could instead charge a $1,000 origination fee, while crediting or otherwise waiving the underwriting and processing charges, provided the $1,000 represented no more than 1% of the loan amount.

For example, a VA borrower is applying for a $300,000 VA loan. There are non-allowable charges attached to the loan, which include:

Underwriting	$500
Processing	$500
Document Preparation	$150
Attorney	$300
Application	$300
Escrow/Closing Fees	$300
Total Restricted Fees	$2,050

The VA lender could instead charge an origination fee of $2,550 and pay the restricted fees directly. Since the $2,550 amount is less than 1% of the $300,000 loan, the entire list of fees may be paid. However, if the fees amounted to more than $3,000, any remaining non-allowable fees must be addressed by the seller or the lender.

Recurring/Prepaid Fees Explained

Recurring fees are an acceptable form of closing costs that the borrower might pay on any VA mortgage loan. These are often called "prepaid fees" and can include items such as an annual insurance premium, a year's property tax bill and prepaid mortgage interest. These allowable fees also involve establishing an escrow or impound account.

An escrow account, or an "impound account" in other areas, is an account established that accrues monthly payments throughout the year and are disbursed when the annual renewal premium is due.

For example, an annual homeowner's insurance policy is $2,400 per year, and annual property taxes are $1,200 per year. Each month, one-twelfth of the annual insurance and property tax bill—or in this instance, $200 per month for insurance and $100 for property taxes—will be included in the house payment to the lender in addition to the principal and interest payment. At the end of the year, the escrow or impound account will have accrued enough funds to pay the annual bills. The lender that has collected the escrow funds will disburse taxes and insurance directly when these are due.

Another recurring prepaid charge is prepaid interest and interest in arrears.

When a mortgage payment is made each month, the amount includes interest that has accrued from the previous month, not for the forthcoming month. For example, if a homeowner makes their payment on July 1, their payment will include 30 days of interest that accrued from the previous month.

Prepaid interest is typically collected on all mortgage loans, both for a refinance and a purchase of a home. For example, you bought a house and the closing takes place on the 30th or the last day of the month. At the closing table, your closing agent will collect interest up to the first of the following month—or, in this example, one day's worth of mortgage interest. If you closed your loan on the 20th of the month, the closing agent will collect interest up to the first of the following month, including the day of closing, or 11 days of interest in this example.

The prepaid interest is collected and forwarded to your new lender, and your first "official" mortgage payment will not be due until the first of the following month in which you closed.

Interest in arrears is the daily amount charged on an outstanding mortgage loan. It is an amount added to the principal balance to calculate a loan payoff. For example, there is an outstanding loan balance of $200,000 during the course of a refinance. The loan will close and officially fund on the 20th of the month. The original mortgage of $200,000 will be paid off during the refinance and will include 20 days of interest from the first day of the current month to the 20th, the day of the closing. If the accrued interest during those 20 days amounts to $1,000, then the payoff amount is $201,000. Furthermore, if a new loan is replacing an old loan, 10 days of prepaid interest will also be collected at the closing table.

Summary

- Closing costs are divided into two categories: one-time charges and recurring charges.

- The funding fee is the only fee charged and required by the VA on all loans.

- The VA restricts certain closing costs that the VA borrower may pay.

- Lenders may charge an origination fee instead of having the VA borrower pay for restricted fees.

5

LOANS 101 - WHAT YOU NEED TO KNOW

This chapter will discuss the basics of mortgage loans, including key components of interest rates, annual percentage rates, loan amortization and equity, among other topics.

After reading this chapter, you will better understand the key components of the critical elements in financing a home with a VA mortgage.

What Is an Interest Rate?

An interest rate is expressed in percentage and represents an amount owed to the lender in exchange for extending a loan to a borrower. If a lender wants to make a return of 8.00% on a loan amount of $10,000 over five years, the lender would receive in exchange for advancing the funds 8.00% on the outstanding loan balance each month until the loan is retired at the end of five years.

The interest rate is one of the four key elements in a mortgage loan calculation. These elements are:

- Length of the Loan (Term)
- Interest Rate
- Loan Amount

- Payment

Mortgage rates are set each business day by mortgage lenders and are so established on a common index. A common misconception regarding mortgage rates is the identity of who sets them and when. The Federal Reserve, or simply "the Fed," is often mistaken as the entity that sets mortgage rates, which is false.

The Fed sets the Federal Funds Rate, which is the rate that banks may borrow from one another over very short periods of time. The Fed also influences the Discount Rate, which is the rate they've established when banks borrow from them directly.

When the Fed raises or lowers rates, the goal is to stimulate or slow down an economy. As funds are cheaper to obtain with lower rates, the theory is that businesses will take advantage of this low cost to borrow money with the purpose of building factories and hiring workers. If an economy is overheated and is growing too quickly, inflation can be a concern. To slow down the economy, the Fed can increase money rates, making it more expensive to borrow money and expand a business.

However, although the Fed does not set your mortgage rate, their actions influence other markets. Technically, a 30-year fixed rate VA mortgage is tied to the Government National Mortgage Association 30-year mortgage-backed security. The Government National Mortgage Association, or "GNMA," is also known as Ginnie Mae. Similarly, a 30-year conventional mortgage underwritten to Fannie Mae guidelines is tied to the Federal National Mortgage Association, or "FNMA" 30-yearr mortgage-backed security (bond).

All lenders set their VA mortgage rates each day on the same index. For example, one lender cannot be at 3.00% while everyone else is at 4.00% – they must all be equal.

Therefore, interest rates are set by individual VA lenders who follow the pricing of the corresponding 30- year GNMA mortgage-backed security. These securities, or bonds, are bought and sold by investors from around the world, as with any other investment vehicle and are traded throughout the day.

As the demand for such bonds increases, the price of that bond goes up. When the price of a bond rises, the interest returned is reduced. Similar securities such as Treasury Bills, CDs and Treasury Bonds follow the same pattern. This would explain why the demand for these securities is higher during a sluggish economy, as investors leave a volatile stock market. In other words, the worse the economy, the lower interest rates will be. The better the economy, the higher the rates.

On the other hand, adjustable rates and hybrid loans are set with its corresponding index. For example, a common adjustable rate index is the 1-year Constant Maturity Treasury (CMT), a publicly traded Treasury bill. When an adjustable rate loan approaches adjustment time, the lender researches the 1-year CMT, adds a margin to it and applies it to the outstanding loan balance.

The mortgage payment does not change until the next adjustment period. A one-year adjustable rate loan can have its rate changed once per year, while a six-month ARM can change once every six months. Most current VA loans that are adjustable loan programs are hybrids, where the initial rate is fixed at the start of the loan term for a predetermined period, such as five or seven years.

Rate Movement

Because mortgage bonds are traded throughout the day, the level of supply and demand can vary. If the variance is too great during a trading day, lenders will adjust their interest rates to reflect the higher or lower pricing of the corresponding index.

This explains why one lender can't have an interest rate that's a full percentage point lower than the rest of the market on the same mortgage loan program. Typical variances in mortgage rates from lender to lender can be between one-eighth to one-quarter percent, as lenders use the same index for their mortgages.

When you see or hear of an interest rate quote in the newspaper, the internet or on the radio, it's possible the rate is no longer available, especially during volatile market swings where investors are unsure of the economy's direction.

When you are shopping for mortgage rates and subsequently getting interest rate quotes, be mindful that what you see or hear as an advertised rate may simply be a rate based on expired data.

The Annual Percentage Rate: the APR

The annual percentage rate, or "APR," is the cost of money borrowed expressed as an annual rate. The APR is disclosed to you by your mortgage lender when you apply for a mortgage loan. It is also a legal requirement all lenders must follow when advertising an interest rate to the public. This requirement was originally established as part of the federal Truth in Lending Act.

The APR is a rate, but it is not your interest rate or note rate, upon which your mortgage payments are calculated. Rather, it reflects additional finance charges associated with an interest rate from a lender.

For example, when you get a mortgage and your rate is 4.00% on a 30-year $200,000 loan, your monthly payment is calculated based on that 4.00% rate. However, lenders are also required to calculate the APR associated with your loan and must take into consideration additional lender fees and finance charges in your monthly payment.

Suppose there are additional finance charges that total $3,000 to get that loan with a 4.00% rate. Those charges could include an underwriting fee, an origination fee, interest charges and other lender-required fees. All VA mortgages will include the funding fee as part of the APR calculation.

Using these figures, the resulting APR would be 4.13%. This is the cost of your money borrowed expressed as an annual rate, which also includes the additional $3,000 in fees required to obtain your 4.00% rate.

So, how does one use the APR? APR is useful when comparing the same mortgage quote from one lender to the next.

Annual percentage rates are a function of term, rate, loan amount, payment, and adding finance charges. Thus, an APR comparison is only useful when comparing the same loan; furthermore, an APR comparison between a 15-year and a 30-year mortgage is useless if you want to find the best deal.

As you compare a lender's interest rate with the APR on your potential loan, you will notice that the APR is higher than the interest rate used to calculate your monthly payment. This is because the APR considers the additional costs required in obtaining your rate; thus, it will always be higher than the interest rate.

The more a lender charges in finance fees, the higher the APR. In the same example shown above, if finance charges were $6,000 instead of $3,000 on a $200,000 mortgage at 4.00%, the resulting APR will be 4.25% – a much higher APR than the 4.13% using only $3,000 in finance charges.

Higher APR will result in higher finance fees. Lenders with a lower variance between the interest rate and the APR will have fewer finance charges than a lender with a higher APR. Again – and this cannot be stressed enough – this APR comparison is only useful when comparing the same loan.

You will see the APR on all mortgage advertisements that include an interest rate quote. As for radio commercials, a lender quotes an interest rate and the loan terms are often quickly detailed at the end in a very fast voice.

If a lender advertises a 4.00% rate in a newspaper ad, you will also see:

- Loan amount used in the ad

- Loan term used in the ad

- The interest rate

- The APR

- Mortgage Operation

Mortgages are a function of loan amount, term and rate. They are also amortized over fixed term as well. Amortization is the method wherein monthly payments are spread out over a fixed period based on the remaining loan balance.

For example, a 30-year fixed rate mortgage on $200,000 at 4.00% results in a principal and interest payment of $954.83. The loan follows the amortization, or payoff schedule over 30 years. The first payment of $954.83 contains both interest to the lender, while the remaining portion is applied to the outstanding principal balance.

In this example, $288.16 is applied to the outstanding (principal) balance and $666.67 toward interest. Exactly 10 years later, that same $954.83 payment applies $429.60 to the outstanding balance with $525.23 to interest. The last payment 30 years later is $951.66 to pay off the loan balance and just $3.17 to interest.

At the beginning of the loan term, more of the payment is applied to interest rather than the loan balance. This is because the loan payment is calculated with 4.00% on a larger loan amount compared to that same calculation made 10 and 30 years down the road. As the loan balance is reduced—or amortized—the lower the interest will be paid to the lender.

As each payment is made toward the principal balance, the outstanding balance is reduced. This results in additional equity for the property, or the amount of the current value of the property that belongs to you—not the lender. Equity refers to the difference between the current value and the amount owed.

For example, if you buy a $200,000 loan and put down 20%, or $40,000, your equity position is $40,000. If you buy a $200,000 home and put nothing down, there is no current equity. However, as each payment is made, your equity grows.

Another way equity is increased is through property appreciation. For example, if you bought that same $200,000 home with zero down but your home increased in value by 10% in one year, the value of the property would be $220,000. Your equity would then be $22,000 by appreciation only:

$$\$220,000 - \$200,00 = \$22,000$$

Let's now look at a combination of both principal reduction and the increasing value of your property due to local market demand.

If your property appreciated 10% over five years and your loan balance naturally amortized down to $171,000, then your equity position in the house would be:

$$\$220,000 - \$171,000 = \$49,000$$

You can have access to this equity in the form of cash with a home equity loan from a lender or you may sell the property for $220,000. In the case of a sale, the outstanding balance is paid off, closing costs associated with the sale are disbursed and the net proceeds go to you. This is your equity.

Equity can also be built by making extra payments toward your principal balance, either as a regular contribution each month or a lump sum.

Summary

- An interest rate is the amount paid to a lender in exchange for borrowing money over time.

- Interest rates are set on an established index, and each mortgage loan program depending on loan term and type can have its own index. Lenders follow the same indexes when setting their mortgage rates each day.

- The APR stands for the "annual percentage rate," which refers to a number that expresses the cost of money you borrowed expressed as an annual rate. The APR considers the interest rate you obtain, the loan term, the amount borrowed, and finance charges required to obtain the loan from a mortgage lender.

- Your monthly payments are based on your note rate, or interest rate and not he APR.

- Mortgages follow a fixed amortization schedule where the loan payments and loan term are set. Each payment contains a portion to the principal balance and a portion to interest payments that are due to the lender. At the earlier stages of a mortgage, more is attributed to interest than toward the end of a mortgage term.

- Equity is the difference between the current value of a home and the outstanding principal balance. Equity can be built by paying down the mortgage, property appreciation or a combination of both.

6

HOUSEHOLD FINANCE 101 - TIPS YOU SHOULD KNOW BEFORE BUYING A HOME

Buying a home is a commitment on many fronts. It's a commitment to your lender to repay the mortgage. It's a commitment to your insurance agent to keep insurance on the property.

Moreover, it's a commitment to pay the property taxes when these are due. But most of all, it's a commitment in solidifying your financial future.

If you surveyed first-time home buyers immediately after they bought their first home, one of the things you'll likely hear is the pride that they now have in owning a home.

Living on your own property is a different feeling entirely compared to living on a rental property owned by someone else. It's exciting—and some even say exhilarating—to sign on closing papers on your first property.

However, without having the proper frame of mind when starting the home buying process as well as determining if you're even ready for such a purchase, home ownership can turn into an ordeal if bills are not paid or it becomes a challenge to pay the mortgage each month.

This chapter will discuss basic financial fundamentals that will put you in the proper frame of mind as well as provide you with financial preparedness to buy your first home with your VA eligibility.

Creating a Budget

A budget is simply a plan for saving, spending and borrowing. Budgets can be highly detailed with each amount spent listed to the penny, or it can be more general.

The purpose of a budget is to ensure you're spending and living within your means while helping you to secure a more stable, profitable future.

A budget consists of the "money in" and "money out" concept. The main source of your "money in" is likely to be a paycheck from your employer or from your business.

Expenses can be categorized in several different areas, and not everyone will have the exact same list. However, all have fixed expenses and floating expenses.

You create your own budget by listing your income and expense accounts, item by item based on expected and actual amount. Below is a basic monthly budget that we will consider.

Income:

Wife's Salary	$5,000
Husband's Salary	$5,000
Total Income	$10,000

Fixed Expenses:

Rent	$2,000
Auto Loan	$500
Student Loan	$100
Insurance	$300
Total	$2,900

Variable Expenses:

Electricity/Gas	$400
Water	$100
Mobile Phone	$250
Cable TV	$150
Food	$400
Gasoline	$250
Entertainment	$300
Clothing	$200
Charity	$300
Total	$2,350
Grand Total Expenses	$5,250
Net Each Month	$4,750

Let's now compare actual expenses with the budgeted expenses. This process can be done each month after all bills are paid to see where your funds are going, the areas on which you can save and how soon it will take to hit your target savings number. In the above example, $4,050 remains after all bills and expenses have been paid.

Income:

Wife's Salary	$5,000
Husband's Salary	$5,000
Total Income	$10,000

Fixed Expenses:

	Budgeted	Actual
Rent	$2,000	$2,000
Auto Loan	$500	$500
Student Loan	$100	$100
Insurance	$300	$300
Total	$2,900	$2,900

Variable Expenses:

	Budgeted	Actual
Electricity/Gas	$400	$480
Water	$100	$150
Mobile Phone	$250	$250
Cable TV	$150	$150
Food	$400	$650
Gasoline	$250	$400
Entertainment	$300	$500
Clothing	$200	$600
Charity	$300	$100
Total	$2,350	$3,280
Grand Total Expenses	$5,250	$6,180
Net Each Month	$4,750	$3,820

In this example, we spent almost $1,000 more than what we had budgeted initially. This means an adjustment in the anticipated amount spent each month must be made and/or a reduction in actual expenses for each item is necessary.

The budget in this example is nevertheless healthy, with $3,820 of discretionary funds still available. Let's now look at the same budget but reduce the income of $10,000 per month to $7,000.

Income:

Wife's Salary	$3,500
Husband's Salary	$3,500
Total Income	$7,000

Fixed Expenses:

	Budgeted	Actual
Rent	$2,000	$2,000
Auto Loan	$500	$500
Student Loan	$100	$100
Insurance	$300	$300
Total	$2,900	$2,900

Variable Expenses:

	Budgeted	Actual
Electricity/Gas	$400	$480
Water	$100	$150
Mobile Phone	$250	$250
Cable TV	$150	$150
Food	$400	$650
Gasoline	$250	$400
Entertainment	$300	$500
Clothing	$200	$600
Charity	$300	$100
Total	$2,350	$3,280
Grand Total Expenses	$5,250	$6,180
Net Each Month	$1,750	$820

When we reduce the income but keep the expenses the same, the net available each month is reduced. While a budget will reveal the movement of your money, it's only the beginning of your budgetary process.

Have you noticed something was missing? What happens if your car breaks down and you need $1,500 in repairs? If you spend your extra funds each month, you can't fix your car. The missing element in the previous example is the amounts dedicated to an emergency fund. However, how much money should you allocate for such an emergency fund?

An emergency fund should contain anywhere from three to six months' worth of living expenses. In this example, three months living expenses falls anywhere between $15,000 to $30,000. That's a lot of money. Nevertheless, it should be your goal to have that amount set aside in an emergency savings account. Some even suggest that more than six months' worth of emergency funds is necessary if you're self-employed.

This three- to six-month fund is available for emergencies such as a temporary layoff or a complete loss of employment. The fund is also meant to take care of unexpected life events that can ultimately occur. Whatever amount you decide to save each month, be it small or large, consider the savings contribution you make each month as an expense or just like any other bill – except in this instance, you're paying yourself.

After your emergency fund has been established, it is time to explore other investment and savings opportunities to help secure your money and to grow.

You should review your monthly budget constantly to see how your money is used and to begin saving for your future—and even to buy your first home.

Another benefit of a budget is it allows you the ability to determine if you're spending within your means. In other words, it refers to spending less than you make. In fact, it is the best way to secure your financial future; spend less money than the amount you make and save the rest.

But what if you don't spend less than you make? The obvious answer is that any savings you may have accumulated will soon be gone, possibly resulting in some serious debt.

Credit Cards

The offers come in the mail. They are offers from credit card companies wanting you to open a credit account with them. After all, it can be used for emergencies, right? Is it not true that you need a credit card for certain things like hotel reservations and other expenses? What about the zero interest rates that some credit card companies offer – those must represent a good thing, right?

Yes, all those things make sense, but financial problems occur when the everyday items that you originally had budgeted are purchased on a credit card and left to be paid later. However, there are many who may use a credit card for specific purchases such as gasoline or business expenses and pay those off entirely each month. The credit card is then a convenient tool in such instances.

After working your budget for several months, do you find that yourself using a credit card instead of your debit card, cash or check to buy something expensive, like a new suit? Maybe you want to go out for dinner with friends and you're already over your budgeted amount for the month. Will you still go out and charge your evening on a credit card, while telling yourself you'll make up for it the next month by not going out as much or at all?

When you find that you're making "deals" with yourself to justify an impulse expense in terms of clothing, entertainment or dining out, that is a warning sign that you may encounter some trouble down the road.

If you have a budget for certain variable expenses and you don't follow it, your financial plan won't work. Worse yet, poor spending habits could leave you with a crippling debt.

Credit is good; however, it must be used properly. For example, if you need a new car and you don't have the $35,000 it takes to purchase it, you may then look for some very competitive car loans. Of course, the best use of credit is for the purchase of a house.

That said, if you find yourself putting everyday items on a credit card rather than using a debit card or cash, or you continue to justify impulse purchases, over time you will seriously damage your financial standing. How do credit card purchases work if you don't pay off the balance each month? Interest accrues. Moreover, if you don't pay the balance due, the balance grows and interest accrues on an even larger balance. If you only pay the minimum amount due each month, that even a $200 charge will take nearly 15 years to pay off.

Credit card companies can charge whatever they want, provided they follow the rules established by the Federal Reserve Board and the newly created Consumer Financial Protection Bureau (CFPB). Such rules determine when and how credit companies can raise or lower your rate, as well as when penalties and interest apply, among a host of other regulations.

Thus, your credit card company can set their own minimum payment amount that you must pay each month. For example, suppose you bought $1,000 plasma screen television and charged it to your credit card because you reasoned that with a credit card, you can pay it off over time. The minimum payment due might be 2.5% per month. With a $1,000 balance on your credit card, that means you will receive your credit bill comes with a minimum monthly payment of $25.00.

But what if your interest rate was 18% and you only paid the minimum balance every month? It would take more than 12 years to pay off that plasma TV. Furthermore, by then, you will have paid more in interest than the television itself, as minimum payments over 12 years would have amounted to more than $1,000 in interest.

Consider now if you continued charging additional purchases on your credit card amounting to another $9,000 over the course of a mere six months. For the sake of this example, one of your recent payments was two days past the due date, so the credit card company boosted your interest rate to 28%.

By only making the minimum payment due, you will pay off your credit card balance in 115 months, or nearly 10 years, while paying nearly $20,000 in interest.

Is There Such a Thing as "Good Debt"?

That's a relative question. Some will tell you that there is no such thing as a good debt and that all debts are a burden and everything you purchase must only be paid with cash. However, the reality is that such practice is not common for most consumers. If there were no such thing as debt, then very few people could purchase a home without financial assistance such as a mortgage. Some college students could not further their education without the assistance of a student loan.

Let's address these types of debt and compare the two. First, interest paid to a lender is an expense just like any other cash outlay you make each month. But mortgages have one inherent advantage that all other debt do not have: income tax benefits.

Mortgage interest is a tax-deductible item on your federal income tax returns. Prior to a major tax overhaul in 1986, many forms of interest from credit purchases were tax deductible, but mortgage interest was the only interest deduction left untouched during such reforms. The only other type of interest that may be tax-deductible is the interest paid on student loans for higher education.

How Does the Mortgage Interest Tax Deduction Work?

As you make your mortgage payments to your lender each month, you will receive a 1099-INT statement from your lender at the end of the calendar year. This statement will show the amount of mortgage interest you paid to the lender for that year.

For example, suppose that you bought a $300,000 house using your VA eligibility and you put zero down. Since this was your first home, your funding fee is 2.15 %, resulting in a $306,450 loan amount. With a 30-year fixed rate at 4.00%, your principal and interest payment calculates to $1,463.04. If you made 12 mortgage payments in the first year, you paid $12,159.77 in interest. That is the amount shown on your 1099-INT.

As you prepare your tax returns, the amount of $12,159.77 will be deducted from your taxable income. That presents huge savings for you. If you made $80,000 that year, you would subtract the interest paid from that amount and your taxable income is reduced to $67,840. With the assumption that you are married and filing jointly, your tax bracket would be 12% for 2018 and going forward. Therefore, it would be $8,140, which represents 12% of $67,840.

It's important to note at this stage that all tax matters should be discussed between you and your accountant or financial planner. This example is not to be construed as tax advice.

The bottom line is that mortgage interest represents a huge amount of savings when it's time to pay Uncle Sam. In this regard, mortgage debt can be considered "good debt."

There are other positive income tax implications when financing a home. If you paid discount points to a lender to buy a home, those points may be tax deductible, as is an origination fee.

Not only does home ownership help solidify your financial future, it helps you keep more of your own money come tax time!

Affordability

This is a question that should be answered by your loan officer. However, in general terms, lenders determine affordability by using debt-to-income ratios, or what is simply known as "debt ratios."

A debt ratio is expressed as a percentage and is determined by dividing your total housing and debt payments with your gross monthly income. The VA debt ratio guideline is 41%, which refers to a debt ratio of 41. If your house payment, car payment and installment loans add up to $4,100 and your gross monthly income is $10,000, then your debt ratio is 41. If your payments total $2,500 and your gross monthly income is $7,000, then your ratio is 36.

VA lenders want to see your debt ratio at or below 41. This does not mean your ratio cannot be higher, like 43 or 44. However, it simply means your loan application will be scrutinized a bit more if your ratio is higher than 41.

What items are included in your debt ratio calculation?

- Your house payment, including principal and interest, taxes, insurance and any HOA fees

- Installment loans, such as an automobile loan, wherein there are more than 10 months of payments remaining

- Minimum revolving credit payments on any outstanding credit card balances

- Child or spousal support payments and child care

For purposes of qualification, lower house payments reduce a debt ratio while higher payments increase it. When you're qualified for a loan amount, a lender will review your current debt loan, current interest rates and current gross monthly income. When interest rates are at their lowest levels, you can qualify for a larger loan compared to when rates were at their highest levels.

Many buyers find out that while they can qualify for a larger mortgage than they anticipated, they decide against getting a loan with a larger amount.

For example, a couple that has been paying $1,500 per month in rent for the past two years discover that their debt ratios allow them to have a house payment at $3,000 per month, which is double what they're used to paying.

The most important aspect of affordability relates to your own comfort level. If you feel comfortable making a specific payment, then share it with your loan officer. Do not let the loan officer dictate the amount you should borrow or the size of the house you wish to buy. That's entirely your decision, not theirs.

Summary

- Create a budget that accounts for all income and expenses
- Establish an emergency fund covering three to six months' worth of expenses, and more if you're self employed
- Spend less than what you make and save the rest
- Stay away from impulse purchases and avoid putting everyday items on a credit card
- Paying only the minimum required payment on a credit card will take you more than 10 years to pay off the debt and will more than double the cost of the purchased item
- Mortgage interest, discount points and origination charges may be tax deductible
- Affordability is determined by your debt ratio, with a maximum debt ratio of 41 as the guideline; however, true affordability depends entirely on you, as well as on your level of comfort.

7

SELECTING A VA LOAN LENDER

The VA does not make mortgage loans. The VA only establishes minimum guidelines that lenders must follow to make a valid VA mortgage loan for a qualified borrower.

Not all lenders are automatically qualified to issue VA mortgages. Those that do originate, underwrite and approve VA home loans must go through an intensive application process prior to doing so.

Despite a mortgage company being approved to do VA home loans, not all their loan officers may have the experience in walking a borrower through the process of a VA application and approval.

VA mortgage loans have their own set of qualification guidelines that do not apply to other loan types, and the documentation and disclosure requirements are different.

It's important to find, not only a mortgage lender qualified to do VA loans, but also a loan officer with VA experience.

Evaluating VA Approved Lenders

To evaluate VA lenders, it is first important to understand the difference between a mortgage lender and a mortgage broker, because both can market themselves as having VA mortgage loans. A mortgage broker does not make a mortgage loan but instead arranges for VA financing between a borrower and a VA lender.

A mortgage broker will meet with you or take an application from you online, prequalify you, gather your documentation then forward your loan file to a VA approved lender. Despite a mortgage broker being a "middleman" in this process, enlisting the help of one does not necessarily mean you will pay higher rates or fees.

A broker has marketing arrangements with various lenders. Such lenders use mortgage brokers to market their mortgages for them. In return for this marketing agreement, these lenders offer slightly reduced rates to the broker, who will then raise the rates to the borrower to meet current market rates.

A mortgage lender is a direct lender. An approved VA lender accepts and evaluates your application, underwrites and documents your application, and provides the funds for your mortgage. The VA lender does everything.

The difference between a broker and a lender is the level of control each has over your loan application. When you work with a mortgage lender directly, the process can be smoother and more efficient. A mortgage broker works both with you as well as the VA lender to help facilitate the transaction. There is no major difference regarding who is better – the broker or the lender.

Rates and fees from either will be similar, yet communication between you and the lender are bridged closer as you are working with the lender directly instead of the third broker, a third party.

As the VA does not issue authority to lenders to underwrite and approve VA mortgage loans, lenders must pass an audit that verifies milestones to be approved to issue VA mortgages. These include a minimum net worth requirement, background checks and a line of credit of at least $1 million, among others,

This special status is what the VA calls "Nonsupervised Automatic Authority". The name itself implies the lender can process, approve and fund VA loans from ordering appraisals without VA involvement, as well as buying and selling VA loans on the secondary market.

Once a lender gets this coveted VA approval, the lender has the authority to perform specific tasks required to get the loan funded, including streamlined appraisal processes and other underwriting privileges.

You can identify if a lender is VA approved by doing some research. Visit the lender's website and look for a VA loan-certified seal, or simply prepare questions specific to your needs once you connect with a lender. In choosing a lender, it is important to note that although a lender has their VA approval, they must have extensive experience in issuing VA home loans.

You want to identify a group of VA lenders that have their own dedicated VA loan department with a loan officer who does nothing but originate, counsel and complete VA loans from start to finish. There are several key points you need to review with a potential VA lender to find one of the best available in the industry.

Rates and Fees

As previously mentioned, the VA does not set rates nor do they set fees charged by third parties. The only fee it sets and collects is your funding fee. Funding fees do not change from lender to lender, so you need not ask a lender what their funding fee is – that fee is established by the VA, not the lender.

Individual lenders are responsible for setting their own interest rates for all mortgage loan products they offer, not just for VA mortgages. In addition, lenders also set their own internal loan fees.

Closing Ratios

A close ratio from a lender's perspective involves the number of loan applications that are taken compared to loans that close successfully.

Also called a "pull through" rate, this ratio is not widely known by the public. An individual loan officer may not even know the exact percentage, but it's something you may ask them.

Successful VA loan lenders should have their goal set to achieve a 100% success rate. It all begins with the individual loan officer evaluating the initial loan application. A loan officer should have the skills to review your income, credit and other factors that may qualify you for a VA loan.

Statistically, a loan application is not complete unless the following five important information are on the application:

- Borrower's Name

- Borrower's Social Security Number (for credit review)

- Income

- Loan Amount

- Property Address

When a borrower begins to search for a home, they must meet with a loan officer for a prequalification. Typically, at this stage, the borrower has yet to find a property. Without a property address, there is no completed application. Nevertheless, the loan officer should determine by this stage whether the potential borrower can qualify for a VA loan or not.

If an experienced loan officer issues the borrower a letter stating that they can qualify for a VA mortgage at a certain amount, then that information should be considered valid.

When a loan that was initially reviewed by a loan officer is later declined, it is likely due to the discovery of a fault or discrepancy during the approval process. For example, the borrower may have claimed to make $10,000 a month on the loan application. Later, after reviewing tax returns, it was discovered he only made $8,000.

A solid closing ratio for a VA lender should be more than 90%. Usually, the two reasons a VA loan may have been declined are because something either changed about the borrower's situation or something was later discovered that made the borrower ineligible for loan approval. However, if nothing is discovered to be amiss about the loan application nor are there changes from start to close, the close ratio should then be 100%. With today's technology, a loan is granted after an initial preapproval upon review of income, credit and necessary documentation. The loan is essentially approved, unless third party information determines otherwise, such as an appraised value being lower than expected.

Another important factor in evaluating potential VA lenders is the length of time the approval process will take. If you're working directly with a mortgage banker who has their non-supervised automatic authority, that's a good start. The next step is to ask where the loan will be processed and underwritten. A loan that is processed and underwritten locally is better than one that is electronically transmitted to a remote facility in another state.

For those living in rural or less populated areas, it's unlikely the lender has an underwriter in your town; however, they may have their underwriter in a nearby city.

Most major retail banks will accept your loan application either online or in their bank lobby. They may, however, send it out for review to a centralized loan processing center.

Such banks may take longer to process and approve a mortgage loan due to the sheer volume of received applications as well the communication issues that can arise from your loan officer and the underwriting department being in separate locations.

If your VA loan can be processed, approved and funded locally by an experienced VA lender, then that lender should be at the top of your list of potential VA lenders.

Efficient and quick processing times are important factors for consideration when choosing a VA lender both for refinancing a mortgage when rates are sensitive and for closing on your VA loan on or before the closing date listed on your sales contract.

Unfortunately, there is no single database of VA lenders available, other than searching for them individually on the internet. You may ask your real estate agent or your friends if they know of a good VA lender. However, a VA loan is not as common as a conventional mortgage, so getting a referral may be more difficult.

Another tried and true method of evaluating a potential lender is to contact the Better Business Bureau and see if there have ever been any complaints listed against a lender.

Evidently, any long-standing business will eventually have a mad customer. Still, the mark of a good business is the way they take care of such a customer. Therefore, if a complaint was made with the Better Business Bureau, how did that lender resolve the issue? Did they ignore the customer?

You can also search for VA lenders on Yelp.com and see if there are any customer comments regarding a specific lender.

Note, however, that with such services as yelp, people who make comments may or may not be a real customer. Anyone can sign up to comment on these sites, and a bad comment may be made by a competitor disguising themselves as an unsatisfied borrower.

Evaluating Your Loan Officer

Your evaluation of your loan officer is most critical during the selection process. A VA lender can be in business for decades and spend thousands on marketing each year, only to have one person—the loan officer—ruin their reputation.

The loan officer is the first person with whom you speak when contacting a lender. They are typically licensed and have gone through an evaluation and training process. However, a loan officer at a VA lender is no different than an employee in any other business. There are good ones and there are bad ones. So, how will you find a good loan officer?

When you searched for a VA lender and asked your questions on rates, fees and closing ratios, it was the loan officer with whom you spoke to. They're the ones with the authority to quote interest rates and fees and prequalify you.

How did you feel when you spoke to this person? Were you comfortable? Were they pleasant? Did they explain things to you in a way you could understand, without sounding condescending?

You will establish a relationship with your loan officer as he will guide you through your approval process. Therefore, you need to like the person with whom you'll be working over the next several weeks.

If a loan officer seems to know their stuff but was rude on the phone or acted as though they had better things to do than talk to you, then you're likely better off finding another company to work with regardless of the status of the VA lender for whom she works.

If you've identified a couple of loan officers at two different VA lenders who are completive in rates and fees, you should then ask them these two basic questions:

- How long have you been a loan officer?
- Do you only work with VA loans?

The length of time a loan officer has been in the industry is telling. A loan officer's job is to not only bring in mortgage loans, but solid loans that can close.

A loan officer is evaluated by his employer based on the amount of production (number of loans) they have brought to the company, as well as his close or pull-through ratio.

If a loan officer does not produce enough loans to justify his employment or the loans brought in are of poor quality and cannot close, it is unlikely the loan officer will survive in the industry. If the loan officer does not produce, he will be fired.

If a loan officer has been in the business for five or more years, it is then established that the loan officer is experienced, works well with his clients and is a top producer for his company.

It's also important to know if the loan officer has any experience with VA loans specifically. While a lender can market VA loans to the public, an individual loan officer needs to bring in mortgage loans of all kinds and may not have extensive experience with VA loans.

If a loan officer answers that they only work with VA loans, this likely indicates that they only want to get your loan in the door. If you're not satisfied with the conviction in the response, ask, "What is my funding fee on this loan?"

A loan officer with any experience will quickly tell you what your funding fee will be. The funding fee is unique to the VA, and if the response is, "I'll get back to you on that," then you've just identified a loan officer with little experience with VA loans.

There are mortgage companies that have VA loan specialists that work with all kinds of VA loans. If your loan officer is one of those specialists, it will be easy for you to tell right away.

You can also find out if a mortgage company has an exclusive VA lending department by placing an anonymous call to the lender and simply asking them, "Who does VA loans at your company?"

A VA loan officer will know their stuff. When you ask questions about the approval process or closing fees, the loan officer's responses will be quick, courteous and thorough.

A loan officer will also return calls promptly, keep their appointments and be patient with you during the interview stage. They will give you their email address, mobile number and all contact information, including that of their manager, loan processor and supporting staff.

If you've gone through these processes in your quest to find a qualified loan officer at a reputable lender, then it is likely you have found your lender.

Summary

- VA loans are distinct from any other loan program, and not all lenders have experience with them.

- VA lenders undergo a rigorous approval process from the VA to obtain the non-supervised automatic authority status.

- A comparison of rates and fees from different VA lenders requires comparing the exact same loan program from one lender to the next.

- In addition to rates and fees, other aspects are important to consider as well, including closing ratios, where the loans are approved and the company's reputation.

- Loan officers should have extensive experience in VA loans and at least five years of experience in the business—the more experience, the better.

8

BUYING A HOME WITH
YOUR VA LOAN

As you embark on your journey in home buying, you will find the process exciting, sometimes confusing and a little scary. That's why it is necessary to take the steps to get you, your team and your finances in order so you'll encounter less stress and enjoy the home search.

The first question you should ask yourself is, "Am I ready?"

Why are you buying a home? Were you told by someone that it was the right thing to do? Did a co-worker just buy a home and you're curious about buying one yourself? Are your parents or relatives urging you to stop renting and put your money to better use?

You must decide on your own if buying a home is the right step for you at this time. It is normal for you to be a bit tentative at first. You will have countless questions, and the numbers, rates and terms you hear will sound foreign to you. Yet, with proper preparation, the home-buying experience can be joyful and not a fearful one.

You must remember that you are the boss throughout this process. You're the one in charge—not your relatives, your real estate agent or not your lender. Real estate agents get paid when they assist in the buying or selling of a home. Loan officers, real estate appraiser and attorneys will also make money.

They will all repeat that same process time and again—it's their job. But this is *your* house. You're the one who will make the mortgage payment every month, not them. What are some important factors to consider?

As you begin scouring the internet for information to begin your research, you will likely see or hear the term "affordability index," which is a general assessment of housing costs, interest rate and median income in a specific geographical area.

This index is a number compared to a baseline of 100. A "70" affordability number for a specific city signifies that 70% of the wage earners in an area can qualify to buy an average price home within that location. An affordability index can be calculated locally, regionally or nationally.

While an affordability index is a number followed by the housing industry, it has less importance for you in your preparing to buy a home. What is important is your very own "affordability index." The affordability index in Kalamazoo does not concern you if you live in Newark.

As discussed previously in Chapter 8, creating and sticking to a budget is important not only to ensure you're living within your means, but that you are also making plans to save enough funds to buy and close on your home.

While VA loans don't require a down payment, there will be closing costs for which you'll need to consider and for which you will pay. You'll also need homeowner's insurance, an appraisal, a credit report and title insurance. Furthermore, you must establish an escrow account. All of that adds up.

You'll want to get a firm handle on the amount of money you'll need to close on a house. Moreover, you'll need to know the remaining amount of money you will have after you close.

When your loan closes, a lender will still want to see at least two months of reserve funds in a liquid account, such as a checking or savings account.

For example, if your principal, interest, tax and insurance payment amounts to $3,000 and the lender requires two months' worth of reserve funds, then you will need $6,000 in your bank account after you've already paid all your closing costs when you close on your home.

If closing costs add up to $5,000 and you need $6,000 in reserves, then you can expect the lender to require at least $11,000 in liquid funds to be in your account for you to receive approval.

To get a better idea for the amount you'll need, contact a VA loan officer and have them prequalify you for a VA loan. They will also provide you with a list of anticipated closing costs and an approximate amount of funds you'll need to close.

Your loan officer will also prequalify you based on your gross monthly income, current installment and revolving debt load. This is reviewed through your debt-to-income ratio.

All mortgage loans carry an inherent debt ratio that lenders follow. For example, suppose your minimum monthly payments are $2,000 and your gross monthly income is $6,000. In that case, your debt ratio is $2,000 divided by $6,000 = .33, or 33. As previously mentioned, the maximum suggested debt ratio for a VA loan is 41. Lenders can approve VA loans above that number, but they might require evidence of available and sufficient discretionary funds or residual income in the bank in the form of additional liquid assets after bills are paid.

A loan officer will look at your gross monthly income and debt, as well as review the current interest rates. Lower interest rates will lower a monthly payment, possibly allowing you to borrow more money.

For example, if your gross monthly household income is $7,000, then the maximum amount that can apply to debt is 41% of $7,000, or $2,870. To calculate VA debt ratios, monthly debt includes installment debt, such as an automobile loan, and revolving debt, such as credit card debt.

Other monthly debt also includes spousal or child support payments and day care expenses. Monthly expenses, such as utility bills, dry cleaners and groceries are not included in this number.

Using the above example wherein $2,870 is the amount for allowable expenses, we will now subtract an automobile payment of $300 and a minimum monthly credit card payment of $70 from that amount. The remaining amount of $2,500 can now be applied toward your house payment. The house payment number includes principal and interest, taxes and insurance.

If the monthly property tax amount is $200 and the monthly estimated insurance is $100, that leaves $2,200 to be applied to principal and interest. A loan officer will then apply a current 30-year fixed rate and calculate for loan amount.

In this example, if the interest rate of 5.00% rate is applied, the approximate loan amount is $409,900.

What can current interest rates do for affordability? If 30-year fixed rates are at 4.00%, the qualifying loan amount is $460,000. If rates are at 3.00%, the loan amount is $521,000. Do you see the difference just one percent in rate can make?

Here is one final note regarding to affordability: Just because you can qualify for a specific amount, it does not mean you're required to take that full loan amount. If a $2,500 per month house payment seems too high for you, take a loan amount that fits you and with which you are comfortable.

The Process

Closing on your new home with your VA mortgage is a process, and each step must be made successfully if you wish to reach your goal of home ownership.

As a veteran or service member, you will first need to determine your eligibility. If this is your first time buying a home and you were honorably discharged or qualified for active duty, your first step is to ensure you're eligible to participate in the program by obtaining your Certificate of Eligibility, or COE.

You may acquire your COE directly from the Department of Veterans Affairs. You will need to provide a copy of your DD-214, complete the request for your COE and send it by mail. However, rather than waiting, an easier method of obtaining your COE is to work with a VA lender who can produce your COE on your behalf electronically within a matter of minutes.

In Chapter 9, we discussed how to find a good VA lender who will help you obtain the necessary paperwork needed to close a VA home loan.

Your lender will also issue your preapproval letter, which is a document from a VA mortgage lender confirming your application for a VA mortgage and that your income, credit and assets have been reviewed and approved. All that is left for you to do is find a property to buy.

Since you've already interviewed and selected a fine real estate agent with your preapproval letter from your lender in hand, the fun part now begins with your search for a new home. Once you've identified the home you wish to buy, your agent will make an offer on your behalf.

The sales price will be negotiated, and once an agreement is made, your lender will order the VA appraisal needed to document the current market value of the home, as evidenced by your sales contract.

You will provide your lender with your most recent paycheck stubs, copies of recent bank statements, tax returns and other necessary financial information. Once your file is documented, it is ready to be sent to the loan underwriter. The underwriter is the person responsible ensuring your loan application conforms to VA guidelines.

After the underwriter is satisfied that your loan meets all the VA loan requirements, the lender will order your closing papers to be sent to your closing agent, who is responsible for ensuring that all of the lender's instructions are carried out completely. This agent will collect funds from you for any outstanding closing costs, prepare the disbursement of funds to all third parties that require payment prior to closing your loan.

Once your loan papers are signed, they will be returned to your lender who will review them to ensure the closing agent followed their instructions. The lender will then contact the closing agent and give their approval to release funds to the seller, third parties and to create your new mortgage loan. When the closing agent disburses all funds, you will have reached the stage called "funding."

The home is then yours.

Summary

- As a home buyer, you are the one in control of the process. People work for you, not the other way around.

- First determine if you're ready for home ownership by finding out the amount for which you can qualify.

- By establishing and following your budget, as well as determining the amount of money you will need to close on a

VA home loan, you can then begin to save the funds necessary in buying a home.

- The loan process begins with determining VA eligibility, which can be streamlined by working with the VA lender you've selected.

- Your VA lender will process, underwrite and print your closing papers to be delivered to your closing agent. Your closing agent will then follow the lender's instructions. When it is determined that the instructions and guidelines have been followed and met, your lender will authorize the closing agent to release funds. At this stage, you're considered a homeowner.

9

FINDING AN AGENT

When shopping for a home, most consumers begin with a casual search on the internet for homes in an area that interests them. Doing so can give you an idea of the neighborhood where you would like to live and the cost of homes within that area. Unless you're an experienced real estate agent, you should use the services of one.

In real estate, the buyer does not pay for the services of a buyer's agent. This agent gets compensated from the seller of the property as part of the sales commissions that is issued to the listing agent who put up the home for sale.

A buyer's agent will help identify not only where you'd like to live, but they can provide you with other information that might be more difficult to find.

At Home Captain, we provide buyers with a pre-screened real estate agent in your area, bringing the most important parties of the home-buying transaction together with a loan officer. Your agent knows more about the real estate market than you ever will.

For example, perhaps there's a neighborhood that interests you, but your agent informs you that a new shopping mall will be built right across the street in the future. Perhaps you are interested in a condominium unit, but your agent advises that the condominium association is constantly involved in some sort of litigation and raises condominium fees to make it more difficult for a potential buyer to obtain financing.

An agent can also provide information regarding neighborhoods close to good public schools if that is one of your priorities. They may also inform you of areas that provide an easier commute to your office compared to other neighborhoods.

Most importantly, the job of a buyer's agent is to represent you throughout the negotiation process when making an offer, evaluating a counter offer and ensuring that all repairs on the property which you're looking at buying are completed to your satisfaction prior to closing.

All of this is free. However, just as there are good and bad loan officers, the same can be said for real estate agents. How do you find a solid buyer's agent? At times, it seems there are real estate agents everywhere, especially when you're in the market for a home. Many agents are part-time. Moreover, most all agents seem to be a "top producer" or a winner of some award or designation.

Good buyer's agents are also good listing agents. As agents begin their careers in real estate, those that excel in the business will eventually have the greatest success. Their longevity in the industry is due to their expertise in real estate, marketing and communication.

An effective way of finding a good agent is to find one that has several homes for sale at the same time. An agent with multiple listings has established a reputation in the industry – they are trusted by both home buyers and sellers simultaneously.

When you announce in your circle that you're thinking of buying a home, you'll likely find that some acquaintances might happen to have a real estate license.

If someone you have known for any length of time hasn't introduced themselves to you as a real estate agent, yet only does so when they discover you're in the market for a home, that agent likely works part-time. If that agent is full-time in the industry and is VA loan certified, you would have known long ago.

The experience or expertise of a buyer's agent with VA mortgages is less of a concern to you when compared to lenders in a mortgage company. While an agent needs to negotiate your buying price and your closing costs, those traits are a staple of all good agents.

You want to find an agent who is active in the market, knowledgeable and with whom you feel comfortable working on your home-buying journey. A quality agent is likely also interviewing you while you are interviewing them. Will you work well together? Are you comfortable with one another? Is the agent aggressive—perhaps even, *too* aggressive? Are they pushy?

As the buyer, are you impatient? Are you too demanding? A good agent will work with those who work well with them. It's certainly a two-way street. However, it is important to remember that you're the one who is in control of the entire process. Nothing will happen unless you make it so.

Where to Start

It is likely you've heard the expression, "Buying a home is the most important financial decision you'll ever make." It's true, but sometimes people hear it so often that it loses its impact. Your real estate agent will walk you through the process; however, you will want your real estate agent to have extensive experience working with buyers who are VA eligible.

Suppose you've already submitted a loan application and supporting documentation and you have your preapproval letter in hand. Your real estate agent won't do too much until you've received this letter. The preapproval letter essentially tells the agent what you can afford, and is a baseline for your home search.

If you don't feel confident with the agents with whom you've spoken and you require a referral, Home Captain can help with its nationwide network of real estate agents who have been prescreened and who have had their reputation verified and who possess hands-on VA home loan experience. All the Home Captain agents are on scorecards with survey feedback from past buyers which influence the agent's rankings. We can't stress enough the importance of working with an agent who knows how to skillfully negotiate your offer. This was covered extensively in the previous chapter.

Suppose that you have your agent and your preapproval letter. You already have a good idea where you want to live. The agent will then take you out to physically visit these properties. However, it is important to be careful and not to let your emotions get the best of you –your agent can help with this. It's too easy to latch onto the first house homebuyers see, especially if they are first time buyers. However, the first home should serve as a benchmark for subsequent homes.

That said, there are real estate markets that are considered extremely healthy; thus, homes sell quickly and you may miss out on a good opportunity. In such "hot" markets, prices continue to rise as buyers compete with one another for the same type of real estate.

Again, that is why working with an experienced real estate agent is critical when you are looking to purchase a home. Perhaps you may have already enlisted the help of a friend or acquaintance who is a real estate agent; however, they must be experienced in representing clients who are using their VA home loan eligibility to buy a home, like those in our Home Captain network.

Summary

- You must find a good real estate agent to work on your behalf. Effective real estate agents can be identified by the many years they have spent working in the business. They must also be constantly working in the market and have several homes listed for sale at any one time.

- Your buyer's agent can help you find the ideal house located in a neighborhood that fits your requirements. They must also consider your future goals when helping you choose a suitable home.

10

REFINANCING YOUR VA LOAN

A refinance loan refers to a loan that "re-finances" an already existing one. A refinance mortgage is a new mortgage and it is not an adjustment or modification of an existing loan. There are different reasons to refinance, with most of them consisting of a readjustment of the interest rate and/or term and the withdrawal of cash equity.

This chapter will cover the many ways of determining whether a refinance loan is advisable in your situation.

When refinancing a mortgage, there is one tried and tested way to determine if interest rates have lowered: You will hear or see advertisements of low interest rates on the radio or on the internet. You will likely hear expressions such as, "Rates are low!" or, "Refinance now!"

Refinancing to a lower rate is the most common reason a homebuyer decides to refinance a mortgage. Lower rates reduce their monthly payment, meaning they will pay less interest to their mortgage company. But how low must rates be to determine if a refinance is a good idea?

One can't simply rely on a variance between their current rate and market rates. A good rule of thumb is that the current interest rate cannot be 1-2% lower than the market rate. While the VA has rules on when a refinance loan is acceptable, the reality is that the monthly payment must be reduced. For this reason, a 1 or 2 percent rule of thumb cannot effectively determine whether a refinance is a good idea. The interest rate is relative to the loan amount.

That means that a 2% drop on a $50,000 loan amount won't have as much of an impact as a 1% drop on a $400,000 loan. The monthly payment amounts are necessary to make a determination; as well as the closing costs associated with the loan.

A refinance mortgage refers to a new loan and will require new closing costs, similar to those incurred when the property was first bought. The VA refinance loan is still subject to the VA's restrictions on the types of closing costs the veteran may pay; however, there are still closing costs which must be addressed.

To determine if a refinance is a good idea, take the difference in your current monthly payment and a new monthly payment obtained with the lower rate, and divide that difference into the closing costs. The result is the number of months it will take to "recover" the closing costs accrued in obtaining the new loan.

For example, suppose you bought a house two years ago. Your current VA mortgage is $200,000, and your rate is 5.00% on a 30-year fixed rate loan. Thus, your principal and interest payment would amount to $1,073 monthly. Current rates available are now lower at 4.00%, which would result in a new monthly payment of $954. Therefore, you will save $119 per month with this new, lower rate.

Suppose that your closing costs add up to $3,000. If you divide $3,000 by your new monthly savings of $119 per month, that leave you with a recovery time of just over two years. Hence, as long as you own and keep that property for at least another two years, then a refinance might be a good idea for you.

Take another scenario, for instance. Suppose you have a loan amount of $50,000 under the same circumstances above. The 5.00% interest rate you had two years ago requires that you make a $268 monthly payment. If rates drop to 4.00% and you refinanced, your new payment is now $238, for savings of $30 per month. If closing costs are $2,000 for a refinance, then $2,000 divided by $30 amounts to five and a half years—that's a long time. Therefore, in this case, refinancing a $50,000 loan is not advisable when the rate only drops by 1%.

Another reason a homebuyer might be inclined to refinance is to change the loan term, specifically from a longer term to a shorter one. The shorter the loan term is, the less interest there will be on a mortgage. Interestingly, a 30-year mortgage can have more than twice the amount of interest over the life of the loan!

Another feature for a rate or rate and term refinance is a cash-out.

A cash-out refinance is a refinance loan where not only are the rate and term adjusted, but the borrower can also pull equity out of the home in the form of cash. For instance, suppose you decide to refinance your $200,000 mortgage with a 5.00% rate to a 4.00%, which would save you $238 per month. But you also decided to pull out another $10,000 to pay off your automobile loan, which has a payment of $300 per month.

Instead of borrowing enough money to pay off the $200,000 loan plus the $3,000 in closing costs, you added another $10,000 to the loan for a $213,000 cash-out refinance. Your payment will increase to $1,016 from $954 at 4.00%. That's an increase of $62. However, it is still much lower than the $1,073 monthly payment you initially had to pay at 5.00%. Furthermore, you paid off your car loan.

VA loans allow for a cash-out refinance, provided the new loan is no more than 90% of the value of the property. Keep in mind, too, that any loan can refinance into a VA mortgage loan, provided the new loan meets all VA guidelines—except for the streamline refinance.

The VA streamline refinance, or the "Interest Rate Refinance Reduction Loan" (IRRRL), is strictly a VA to VA loan, meaning only an existing VA loan qualifies for a streamline status.

A streamline loan requires much less documentation. No employment history, income verification or credit check are required. The only stipulation is that there is no evidence of any late payments of more than 30 days past the due date in the most recent 12-month period. The streamline also has fewer closing costs.

Summary

- Replacing an existing loan with a new loan is called a "refinance" loan.

- Refinancing can be beneficial when reducing the interest rate and/or the loan term.

- Calculating the recovery period is a way to determine if a refinance is a good idea.

- Any loan can be refinanced into a VA mortgage loan, except a streamline refinance.

- A streamline refinance is strictly a VA to VA loan program, with reduced closing costs and documentation requirements.

11

FINANCIAL REQUIREMENTS
FOR A VA LOAN

VA loans require that basic qualification guidelines be followed regarding credit and credit scores, qualifying income, debt and debt ratios, and employment history.

Credit and Credit Scores

Credit is an essential factor lenders evaluate in a VA loan request. While the VA does not establish a minimum credit score, lenders have set their own guidelines for credit and credit scoring.

Credit relates to a consumer's ability and willingness to repay a debt. "Ability" refers to their having sufficient income to make the monthly payments on any acquired debt, while "willingness" refers to the consumer's agreement to make payments when these are due. Over time, a credit history is established, which will indicate a borrower's credit eligibility.

Credit scores take the form of a number that indicates the likelihood that a borrower defaults on a debt. This number can range anywhere from 300 to 850, and it is the result of an algorithm developed by a company called Fair Isaacs Corporation, or FICO. The terms "FICO score" and "credit score" are interchangeable.

A credit score evaluates a consumer's recent credit history, with more emphasis on the most recent two-year period. Credit scores refer to a consumers' past payment history, available credit, age of credit history, new credit and inquiries, and the types of credit the consumer has used or is using.

The first two categories, payment history and available credit, account for nearly two-thirds of the entire credit score, with the remaining three categories accounting for the other one-third. If a consumer makes payments on time and is never late, their credit score will rise. If a consumer uses credit responsibly and typically only uses approximately one-third of their available credit, their scores will again rise.

However, if a late payment is made or a consumer borrows above the credit line, their scores will begin to fall. Credit scores are dynamic and will change throughout the consumer's life.

There are three credit reporting agencies: Equifax, Experian and TransUnion. All report FICO scores to lenders at the lender's request. The result is three credit scores, and the lender will use the middle score for evaluation purposes.

Most VA lenders have established the minimum credit score of 620 for a borrower to qualify for a VA loan. If their credit score is 619, the lender is under no obligation to approve the loan, and the borrower must repair the credit before re-applying for a VA loan again in the future.

Sometimes, however, the lender may still consider the loan request from a borrower without a score or with a low credit score.

When a borrower has a loan application and there is no qualifying credit score on file, some VA lenders will choose to perform what is called a "manual underwrite," wherein the loan application is evaluated independent of an automated approval from an established automated underwriting system, or AUS.

An AUS is an online loan submission and evaluation program that accepts a loan application electronically, reviews the loan file and issues an approval to the lender. Provided the lender follows the instructions issued by the AUS, the loan can be approved and funded by the lender. The AUS approval typically sends approval instructions within seconds after a lender submits the electronic file.

However, if there is no credit score in the loan file or the credit score is below lender requirements, an automated approval is not possible. A lender will perform a "manual underwrite" by individually reviewing income, assets and credit history to grant a loan approval.

A manually underwritten loan requires evidence of compensating factors associated with the loan file that can override a low or non-existing credit score. For example, a borrower's credit score may be low due to a recent divorce or catastrophic life event; however, the borrower previously had a significant amount of savings accumulated over the years or had a solid income and low debt ratios. Compensating factors can consist of several elements, but they must weigh heavily enough to sway the lender's decision for loan approval. After all, lenders are required to determine if the borrower has the ability and willingness to repay a debt.

When lenders review a VA loan application, they look at gross monthly income from all borrowers on the loan, which refers to all income before any deductions are taken.

Income can come in several forms. However, income that qualifies for a VA loan approval are:

- Employee Pay
- Bonus Pay
- Commission Income
- Self-Employment Income
- Interest and Dividends

- Social Security and Retirement
- Spousal Support Payments

Employee pay is the pay an employee receives from their employer. Proof of employee pay can be evidenced by two of the employee's most recent paycheck stubs covering at least a 30-day period, as well as recent W2 forms and tax returns from the last two years.

Bonus pay, as well as commission income, can be used as proof of income for loan approval if the bonus or commission income is made regularly, can be verified as having been received over the previous two years, and can be expected to continue for the next three years.

Self-employment income can also be used if proof of such income has a two-year history, evidenced by two tax returns from the last two years and can be supported by business bank statements.

Interest and dividend income may be used if there is a two-year history of the income and can be expected to continue for at least three years. Copies of the last three months' investment statements are required.

Social security and retirement income may be used if the income can be documented and show the likelihood of continuation for at least another three years.

Spousal support payments can be used if there is a two-year history of regular payments received, and there is proof of likelihood that it will carry on for at least another three years.

Service pay for active duty personnel is acceptable if there is at least a two-year history of serving, and the borrower has completed at least 181 days of service.

Debt

When reviewing debt, lenders will count the required minimum monthly payments from all revolving, installment and obligated debts paid for each month.

Qualified debt includes minimum payments on credit card balances, and installment debt on automobile or equipment loans. Installment debt with less than 10 months of payment remaining will not be considered as a debt, given the outstanding installment debt will soon be retired.

If there are any spousal or child support payments the borrower pays every month, those debts will be counted, provided the debts are to be paid for at least three more years. This is evidenced by a review of the copies of the signed divorce decree, which show the amount and duration of the support payments.

Any other monthly obligation, such as income tax payments or other installment plans, will also be considered as debt.

Payments for consumer items such as food and entertainment are not counted, nor are other everyday expense items, such as clothing and utility bills.

The final debt that is used to evaluate a VA mortgage application is the debt to be incurred on the new VA mortgage loan. The items included in the new house payment include the principal and interest payment on the new mortgage, the monthly property tax and insurance payment, and any homeowner's association or condominium fees that are to be paid monthly.

Lenders review income and debt to calculate the debt ratio, set at 41. As discussed in previous chapters, the debt ratio is calculated by dividing the qualifying monthly debt by the total gross monthly income. Therefore, if the monthly debt is $3,000 and the income is $9,000, the debt ratio would then be 33, as the following formula applies:

$3,000 divided by $9,000 = .33, or 33.

This 41 debt ratio is the standard, but debt ratios may be a bit higher, typically as high as 45. If a lender approves a loan with a debt ratio higher than 41 but lower than 45, the lender will highlight in the loan application the compensating factors taken into consideration to approve the loan. For example, a borrower has a debt ratio of 44, but the borrower has a high credit score of 800. This high credit score may be considered the compensating factor by the lender to approve the loan.

Another strong compensating factor is job and employment history. A VA loan needs to show a two-year history of full-time employment, preferably in the same line of work in a single company.

If an employee has worked five years for his employer and has seen his income steadily increase, then the borrower has demonstrated job stability. However, if a borrower has spotty employment history, gaps in employment and multiple employers over the recent years, then the loan may not be approved without proper and adequate explanation provided by the borrower.

Summary

- The financial requirements for a VA loan include a good credit and a minimum credit score of 620

- If a credit score is not available or below 620, a lender may choose to underwrite the loan manually without the benefit of an automated approval system (AUS)

- VA lenders have specific requirements for qualifying income and qualifying debt

- Debt ratios for VA loans are limited to 41 but may go higher with compensating factors in the loan file. Most lenders will not approve any VA loan with ratios above 45.

- Full-time employment history and evidence of job stability are important factors when evaluating a VA loan application. Spotty or part-time employment can hurt the borrower's chances for approval.

12

VA LOAN POLICIES

In addition to the financial requirements in a VA loan application, the VA has also established general loan approval guidelines and features inherent in a VA mortgage. All lenders who issue a VA mortgage must follow these policies properly to issue a qualified VA home loan. These policies address loan characteristics such as loan limits, entitlement, occupancy and special policies addressing short sales and bankruptcies.

Loan Limits and Entitlement

The VA is not responsible for issuing a maximum VA loan, but lenders will generally limit a VA loan to $453,100, which coincides with the current conventional loan's maximum amount. The VA will issue a loan guarantee to the lender that equals 25% of the total loan amount.

This limit is issued based on the borrower's basic entitlement, which is currently set at $36,000. The VA will guarantee four times that amount to a lender, or up to $104,250 for loans above $144,000.

Yet this calculation is outdated and only applies to calculations on partial entitlement. As mentioned in a previous chapter, the VA loan limits follow those set forth by Fannie Mae and Freddie Mac and can adjust each year.

VA loan limits may also be higher depending on the location of the property in so-called "high cost" areas such as Hawaii, Guam,

Alaska, and parts of California, Florida, New York and others. The VA publishes these limits by county on their website.

When a veteran begins the VA home loan process, it is important for them to remember that eligibility is determined by their certificate of eligibility from the VA. This certificate will not only indicate their eligibility, but also their available entitlement amount. If the veteran has never used the entitlement, the amount will be $36,000.

It is possible, although uncommon, for a veteran to use only part of his entitlement, only to use the remaining amount to purchase another property. However, it is important to note that VA loans can only be used for a primary residence and therefore cannot be used for investment properties.

Still, a veteran can use part of his entitlement to purchase a primary residence then later move out of the house. They may then rent it out before buying a new primary residence.

For example, a veteran used part of his entitlement a few years ago. His original entitlement was $36,000, but he only used $18,000 to buy a $72,000 condo.

Later, he decides to move out of his condo, rent it out and buy another home. His remaining entitlement of $18,000 means the VA will guarantee four times that amount to a VA lender, or $72,000.

The veteran can find a $72,000 home without putting any money down and still qualify for a VA mortgage. Any sales price above the $72,000 guarantee will require a down payment of 25% of the difference between the sales price and the loan guarantee.

As you can see, the use of partial entitlements is rare and unlikely in today's environment, as most homes sold are well above any remaining entitlement that could be used for a zero down VA loan. Nevertheless, it is still possible for a borrower to have two outstanding VA loans at the same time.

A more common scenario is one wherein a borrower with a VA loan sells the property and pays off the existing VA home loan. This indicates the original entitlement is restored back to the original level. Sometimes, however, the VA might not receive information that the prior VA loan had been paid off during a sale and thus fails to restore the entitlement.

If a qualified borrower obtains the certificate of eligibility for a subsequent use of the entitlement yet the certificate indicates no available entitlement, the veteran can then contact the VA directly and provide a completed 26-1880 form to have the entitlement restored. Yet, as with most aspects regarding the VA loan program, the VA lender can streamline this process for you entirely.

All that is typically required to restore entitlement is evidence that the property was sold and payments made to pay off the previous VA loan. VA loans can also be restored if a conventional loan is used to refinance out of a VA mortgage.

Finally, a recent policy change has been implemented for VA loans in light of the recent economic downturn; it addresses short sales and bankruptcies, which can both negatively affect a credit score.

A short sale is when a VA-financed property is sold, but not for an adequate amount required to pay off the old VA mortgage. For example, suppose the outstanding mortgage of the sold house is $200,000 but the property only sold for $150,000. Therefore, this results in the payoff being short by $50,000.

A lender can accept a short sale offer that would allow the loan to be paid off entirely for the $150k amount; this would not include the total outstanding balance, and the loan would be considered completely retired. A short sale is usually the last option to avoid a foreclosure and bankruptcy.

If a VA borrower has a recent bankruptcy, foreclosure or short sale, there are specific waiting periods they must respect before a new VA loan can be issued to them.

If there is a bankruptcy discharge, the veteran must wait two years from the discharge date for a Chapter 7 bankruptcy filing and one year from the completion of a Chapter 13 bankruptcy.

The foreclosure waiting period is two years from the date the property was foreclosed and transferred back to the bank.

A short sale waiting period is two years from the date the sale took place. However, there is no waiting period at all in the instance of a short sale if the borrower had no mortgage late payments during the preceding 12-month period prior to the short sale taking place.

In all three scenarios, reestablished credit must be verified before a VA loan can be considered.

Summary

- The VA sets additional loan policy guidelines in addition to financial considerations.

- The VA does not set individual loan limits for VA lenders but guarantees up to four times the amount of the qualifying veteran's available entitlement, or 25% of the loan amount if the loan exceeds $144,000.

- VA borrowers may have more than one VA loan at a time depending on available entitlement.

- VA loans are made for a primary residence only.

- Entitlements can be restored by paying off the outstanding VA loan.

- The VA requires specific waiting periods after catastrophic financial events such as bankruptcies, short sales or foreclosures before a new VA loan can be issued.

13

FINANCIAL AND TAX STRATEGIES

Owning and financing a home with a VA mortgage offers favorable income tax considerations in addition to helping establish a more solid financial future with real estate equity. This chapter provides general advice regarding income tax strategies; however, it should not to be considered professional tax or investment advice.

There are specific tax deductions afforded to those who own and finance a home that are not available for tenants. Income tax deductions are amounts that can be deducted from a taxpayer's gross income to reduce overall tax liability. Homeowners can deduct the interest paid on their loans along with property taxes, which can help to offset the cost of house payments and reduce the homeowner's tax burden.

For example, imagine a couple that makes $75,000 a year and itemizes deductions. There is a multitude of possible income tax deductions that include items such as school supplies bought by a teacher for work-related reasons or donations made to charity – these can be deducted from gross taxable income. Let's see how owning a home can offset income tax bills using a $75,000 annual income as an example. This amount puts the couple in the 25% tax bracket. This translates to an initial tax bill of $75000 or $18750 owed in taxes. Next, we will consider the effects of tax deductions on a $250,000 loan financed at 4%. Mortgage interest is tax-deductible, and in the first year, there was $9,919 in interest paid to the lender. Instead of the income tax rate being applied to $75,000, the tax is applied to $65,081, the taxable amount after mortgage interest has been subtracted from the annual income.

Property taxes are also a tax-deductible item; therefore, if property taxes were $2,500 in the past income tax year, then $2,500 is also deducted from taxable income. Thus, it lowers the amount of taxable income to $62,581. In this scenario, the result would bring the taxable income down to a lower tax bracket from 25% down to 15% – the income tax now becomes 15 % of $62,581, or $9,387! That represents less than half the original tax bill!

However, it should be noted that the above scenario is a hypothetical example and does not take into consideration other tax deductions, such as personal and dependent deductions, medical and other tax considerations. All tax questions should be addressed to a tax professional. Nevertheless, the effect of mortgage interest deduction is undeniable. Mortgage loans that qualify for deductible interest from gross income are restricted to owner-occupied properties and second homes. Second homes refer to vacation homes that are not rented out for more than two weeks each year. Any property that is owned by the veteran and is rented out for more than two weeks per year is considered an investment property. Evidence of rent money received, as well as mortgage interest, taxes, and insurance paid, can be found in personal federal income tax returns. Qualifying owner-occupied and second home properties include single-family homes and any owner-occupied duplex, triplex, or fourplex. A veteran can live in one of the units in a fourplex and the property can still be considered a primary residence.

Another financial attraction associated with owning your own home is the amount of equity that builds up over the term of the loan. As each mortgage payment is made, a portion goes toward paying interest while another is paid directly toward the outstanding mortgage balance. The difference between the current value of the property and the outstanding mortgage is called the owner's equity. For example, if a home is valued at $200,000 and the outstanding loan balance is $150,000, then the owner's equity is $50,000. This would be the approximate amount the owner will receive should the owner decide to sell, minus applicable selling costs. This equity can also be issued to the owner in the form of cash in the form of cash without selling the property; a loan issued against the current equity in the property is known as an equity loan.

Equity is gradually built up over time as payments are made each month, which resembles a forced savings account. Equity can also be attained through natural property appreciation. Suppose an owner's property is valued today at $250,000 and appreciates 5% over the next year to a value of $262,500. If the outstanding loan balance is $200,000 and falls to $192,000 one year later, the equity in the property is $70,500 on a $262,500 value. Equity increases as the loan balance is reduced and/or as the property increases in value.

Summary

- There are significant financial advantages to owning and financing a home rather than renting.

- Mortgage interest and property taxes can be deducted from taxable income to reduce income tax liability.

- Equity is the difference between the value of a property and the outstanding loan balance.

- Property appreciation and loan balance reduction automatically contribute to the owner's overall financial net worth.

14

LOAN STRATEGIES

There are several types of VA loans, each with its own set of characteristics and guidelines. Interest rates and monthly payments can vary based on different variables, and the veteran can choose from any that will meet qualifying criteria. This chapter will discuss these different options and ways they can be applied in various situations. These different loan characteristics are:

- Loan Term
- Loan Type
- Loan Purpose

Loan Term

VA mortgage loans can carry different payoff or amortization periods. These periods can be as short as ten years, or as long as thirty years. However, there are other term choices available in five-year increments: 20- and 25-year terms. The longer the term, the lower the monthly payment; the shorter the term, the less interest will be paid over the life of the loan. Let's look at the different loan terms and consider the difference between monthly payments and interest paid over the term of the loan. In all examples, the fixed rate will be 4% on a $300,000 loan.

Term	Payment	Interest Paid
30	$1,432	$275,520
25	$1,583	$174,900
20	$1,817	$136,080
15	$2,219	$99,431
10	$3,037	$64,440

Based on this chart, you'll notice right away that the longer the loan term, the lower the monthly payment is. However, at the same time, the longer the loan term, the more interest is paid to the lender.

Loan Type

The different loan types are fixed rate loans, adjustable rate mortgages (ARM), and hybrids. A fixed rate has a rate that stays the same throughout the life of the loan, so the payment amount does not change. An adjustable rate mortgage, or ARM, is a loan program in which the interest rate can change based on a predetermined set of rules. We talked about adjustable rate mortgages briefly in an earlier chapter; we will now examine these in detail.

An ARM has five basic components:

- Index
- Margin
- Adjustment Period
- Adjustment Cap
- Lifetime Cap

An ARM rate is comprised of a margin added to an index. The index can be any common financial instrument such as a one-year treasury bill or prime rate. The margin refers to a percentage added to the index. The index for a VA home loan can be either 2 or 2.25%, depending on the nature of the loan.

The adjustment period is the predetermined date at which an interest rate can be adjusted. A one-year ARM can adjust only once per year, whereas a six-month ARM can adjust every six months, and so forth. For example, if a one-year ARM was to adjust today and the index was 1.5 % and the margin 2%, the new rate until the next adjustment would be 3.5%.

The adjustment cap and the lifetime cap are consumer protection features that limit how high the adjustment can be at each adjustment period as well as over the lifespan of the loan. The adjustment cap limits how high a rate can be at each adjustment, whereas the lifetime cap limits how high the rate can be over the life of the loan.

A one-year VA ARM will have a 1% annual cap and a limit of 5% over the initial rate in the life of the loan. For example, if the rate was to adjust today and the one-year treasury index was 7%, then the rate should now technically be 9%. However, due to the lifetime cap, the rate could never go beyond 5% above the starting rate. If the starting rate was 2.5%, the rate could never get higher than 7.5%, regardless of what the index might be. Furthermore, the adjustment cap would limit any adjustment at 1% above the previous year's rate. A hybrid mortgage is in essence a form of ARM, but it is fixed for the first three to five years before it turns into an ARM which is after the initial fixed period. Hybrids can offer slightly lower start rates compared to fixed rate mortgage loans.

Loan Purpose

A VA loan can be used to finance a purchase or to replace an existing loan. In these instances, it is referred to as a refinance. A refinance loan can be used to reduce the interest rate and adjust the term, or to adjust the rate and term while also pulling out some equity from the property in the form of cash. This type of refinance is called a cash-out refinance.

As interest rates fluctuate year after year, interest rates can drop to levels below what they were just a few months or years ago. If you financed your VA mortgage two years ago and the 30-year rate was 5% but rates are now 3.5%, then your monthly payments would be reduced.

On a $200,000 mortgage at 5%, the payment is $1,610. The payment with a 3.5% rate is $1,347, for a monthly savings of $263. You can refinance any loan into a VA refinance loan, provided you do not pull out any cash during the transaction and you meet the underwriter guidelines.

The Interest Rate Reduction Refinance Loan (IRRRL) is a streamlined version of a traditional VA refinance. The streamline refinance loan requires less paperwork, less documentation, and has reduced fees. The streamline loan is only available when a VA loan is refinanced into a new VA loan, or a VA-to-VA transaction.

By using the above example with a cash-out refinance, you can withdraw additional funds with a VA cash-out refinance loan of up to 90% of the current value of the property. Although you are allowed 100%, many lenders only allow for 90 percent in a cash-out refinance.

If the property was appraised at $250,000 and you selected a cash-out refinance loan at 3.5% with a loan amount of $225,000, you could pay off the old mortgage with the 5% rate, pay the closing costs associated with the new loan, and take home approximately $20,000 in cash with which you may do whatever you please.

After reviewing the different loan terms, types, and purposes, what are the advantages of each?

Fixed rate loans provide the most security compared to an ARM or a hybrid. Because the payment and rate never changes, it is the most stable of the three.

When deciding on the fixed rate loan term, consider taking the shortest term to reduce the amount of interest paid each month and over the life of the loan that also keeps your mortgage payment within acceptable debt ratio guidelines.

The least interest to be paid is over a ten-year period, but that period also has the highest amount for monthly payments. It is so high that a shorter term could push your debt ratio too high to even be approved.

Borrowers should consider an adjustable rate mortgage if they know at the time of financing that they will sell their home or otherwise retire the mortgage due to other reasons, such as a job transfer.

Adjustable rate mortgages, which might be the loan of choice in such instances as ARM rates, will typically be lower in the beginning compared to fixed rate mortgages.

A hybrid loan falls between a fixed rate loan and an ARM. It can offer the stability of a fixed rate mortgage for the initial three-, five-, seven- to ten-year period before turning into a more unstable adjustable rate mortgage.

When Not to Choose a VA Loan

VA mortgage loans carry similar loan options compared to other loan types, including term, type, and purpose. Despite the VA mortgage loan being the best loan program for qualified borrowers with little or no money down, a VA loan is sometimes not the best option for a homebuyer.

While VA mortgage rates are competitive with any other mortgage program, VA home loans carry an additional fee that conventional mortgage programs do not: the funding fee.

We discussed the funding fee in detail in Chapter 6. To summarize, except VA loans for those with a service-related disability, the funding fee is still required at 2.15% of the loan amount for a first-time purchase and higher for others.

For a home loan of $300,000, that means an additional fee of $6,450. While the funding fee can be rolled into the VA loan, it is still an additional cost that must be paid for, either out-of-pocket or over time.

If the borrower has a 20% down payment, then a conventional loan is likely the best choice, all things being equal. Even with a 20 percent down payment, a VA loan will have a funding fee nevertheless. In cases like this, the conventional mortgage is the best answer.

Moreover, while the VA does not prohibit construction loans, few if any lenders will issue a VA-guaranteed construction loan. A better alternative is a standard construction loan from a bank.

At the end of the construction term, the construction loan will need to be replaced with a permanent mortgage, which can be a VA loan or a conventional loan.

If the value of the home exceeds the construction loan by 20% by the time construction is completed, then a conventional mortgage is likely the better alternative.

If the value of the renovated home is at or near the construction loan amount, then the VA loan might be the better choice.

Summary

- VA mortgage loans are categorized by term, type, and purpose.

- For loans with lower payments, a longer loan term is best. For loans with less interest paid, shorter loan terms are better.

- Adjustable rate mortgages (ARMs), offer lower starting rates compared to fixed rate loans; however, they can vary in payment throughout the life of the loan. Rate adjustments are accompanied by interest rate caps that limit how high an interest rate can be at any adjustment period and over the life of the loan.

- A hybrid loan is an ARM that is fixed for the first three to five years, depending on the nature of the hybrid. After the initial fixed term of the hybrid, the loan turns into an ARM with annual adjustments.

- Refinance loans can be requested to lower a rate and/or adjust a term. A cash-out refinance loan is used to adjust the rate or term simultaneously, pulling out equity in the form of cash.

- If a homebuyer has any funds available for a down payment funds, a VA mortgage may not be the best option for them due to the VA funding fee. In the case of down payment or additional equity, a conventional loan might be the better choice.

15

VA LOANS AND INVESTMENT PROPERTY

The VA has established that the VA home loan benefit may only be used for primary residences. This means the homebuyer must live in and occupy the property as their home. VA loans cannot be used to buy investment or rental properties. Nevertheless, it is still possible to combine VA financing and investment properties in certain cases.

There are two primary ways a VA loan can be associated with an investment or rental property. The first is by using a VA loan to purchase a primary residence, and then after living in the property for some time, buying a larger home while keeping the first property, as well as the VA mortgage intact.

This is not an uncommon practice at all, especially for those who use their VA entitlement to buy their first home when down payment and closing cost funds are hard to come by.

Later, as the veteran's family grows or an upgrade to a larger home is necessary and savings accounts have been established, the borrower may obtain a conventional loan with a down payment. This is perfectly legitimate in the eyes of the VA, as the initial loan approval was based on the veteran's initial intention to occupy the purchased property. Loan approvals are issued based on current intent and not future possibilities.

For veterans who keep a house with a VA loan in place and who wish to buy an additional home, there are some factors that require their consideration before they can complete such a transaction.

The first hurdle is the ability to qualify with two mortgages—the old mortgage and the new one. For example, suppose the current VA mortgage monthly payment is $2,000 and the new mortgage will be $2,500 per month. That is a total of $4,500 in housing payments alone.

In this example, the borrower does not have any remaining entitlement and has chosen to obtain conventional financing for the new property. They must keep in mind that conventional loans have their own guidelines regarding rental income.

Conventional debt ratios are like VA debt ratios, with the maximum allowable debt ratio being 45 although this number can change from lender to lender. A maximum 45 debt ratio signifies that the monthly debt divided by gross monthly income cannot exceed 45 in most circumstances. In this example, the borrower would have to earn $10,000 per month to qualify for the new mortgage. That number is calculated by the following formula:

$$\$4,500 \ / \ \$10,000 = 45$$

If the borrower can qualify for the new mortgage while carrying both loans with $10,000 in income per month, the transaction may likely be approved. However, if the borrower cannot qualify for both mortgages without the support of rental income from the existing property, there are specific guidelines that need to be followed.

If the borrower does not make enough capital each month to qualify for both mortgages and rental income from the existing home needed to qualify, the conventional loan will have some additional requirements from the borrower.

Suppose the borrower makes $7,500 per month and the borrower's total qualifying monthly debt is $3,000. The debt ratio in this example would be 40, and anything under this ratio is likely to be approved for conventional loans.

Yet, the borrower's existing mortgage of $2,000 still needs to be accounted for. Therefore, by adding that amount to the current debt, the total debt becomes $5,000, causing debt ratios to skyrocket from 40 to 67. This in turn results in the loan being denied without accounting for rental income.

However, rental income from the existing property may be used to help the borrower qualify nonetheless, provided the following specific conditions are met:

- There is an existing lease signed by the new renters

- A copy of a cancelled check or cashier's check made out from the renter to the owner exists

- The borrower has had landlord experience in the past

The last requirement is typically the most difficult to criterion of qualification—either the borrower has had landlord experience in the past or not. The landlord experience does not necessarily have to be recent, but it must be verified.

Landlord experience verification is completed with a review of the previous year's tax returns (which show rental income and expenses on the borrower's returns), along with a copy of the prior lease agreement. If landlord experience can be established, then the loan application can proceed.

To determine rental income, the lender will take the rental income listed on the lease agreement and multiply it by a factor of .75. This multiplier is used to offset maintenance charges and vacancies that may occur throughout the lease period. In other words, only 75% of the rental income proceeds count.

If the $2,000 on the existing VA mortgage, which includes principal and interest, taxes, and insurance in addition to any homeowner's association dues, can be offset by rental income, the borrower may qualify for the new mortgage. Below are the resulting debt ratios based on rent shown on the new lease agreement in our example:

Mortgage	If Rent is:	.75	Net
$2,000	$2,000	$1,500	$500
$2,000	$2,500	$1,875	$125
$2,000	$3,000	$2,250	$225

This chart shows the impact the amount of rent can have after applying the .75 multiplier, indicating if the rental cash flow is positive or negative. You will notice right away that if the rent charge is the same as the existing house payment, the lender will view this as a net loss of $500 each month.

Notice in this example that it is only when the rent is $3,000 or more that the rental income completely offsets the existing mortgage payment of $2,000.

When a lender sees a net loss on a rental, the lender will simply add that net loss to the monthly debt load. If the rent is only $2,000 per month, the lender will add the $500 loss to the borrower's debt ratios. If the ratios are still in line, then the loan may be approved; if not, the veteran may need to increase rent or request a lesser loan amount to finance the new property.

While most loans require previous landlord experience, this requirement may be waived in some instances, when the following conditions have been met:

- The existing property has at least 30 percent equity.

- The borrower has at least six months of payment reserves for both properties.

Suppose the home the veteran is leaving behind has a current loan balance of $150,000. The new lender can order an appraisal on that property. If the property appraises for at least $215,000, which shows at least 30 percent equity, the veteran has met the first requirement.

Next, the veteran must show a minimum of six months' worth of reserves in the form of cash or liquid assets to cover both the old mortgage and the new one for which they are applying. If the old mortgage is $1,500 per month and the new mortgage is $2,000 per month, then the new lender will want to verify six months of reserves for both accounts. In this example, that amounts to $21,000 left over after the new home closes.

$$(\$1500 \times 6) + (\$2000 \times 6) = \$21,000$$

If your situation meets these requirements, then a lender may waive the landlord experience requirement.

Multi-Family Property

Another way to use your VA entitlement for investment property is to purchase a duplex or other multi-family property with no more than four units, while living in one of these units. The most common instance of this practice is a situation wherein the veteran buys a duplex and uses the rental income to offset part or all of the new mortgage. While the VA does not issue loan limits, VA lenders do. Furthermore, the VA will guarantee a mortgage for a multi-family property up to $453,100, higher in certain "high cost" areas.

Standard VA guidelines apply when financing such properties, and the loan is underwritten in the same manner.

The VA allows you to purchase a multi-family unit with no money down and reduced closing fees, along with the same competitive rates as any other VA loan. The VA home loan will also allow you to use your rental income to qualify for the mortgage, should you need the additional income to meet certain conditions.

VA guidelines require that you have had previous landlord experience or additional compensating factors to offset the mortgages if you are inexperienced in it. This allowance for additional compensating factors is dependent on the individual VA lender approving the loan. Such factors may include an excellent credit history, significant assets, and others.

If the lender with whom you wish to work allows the use of the rental income to be obtained from property, the lender will apply 75 percent of the income to your gross monthly income for qualification purposes. The lender will want to independently verify the amount of rent that is being paid each month, typically with a copy of a lease agreement. However, the lender will also use the information taken from the individual appraisal used to assist in the underwriting process.

The appraisal, which helps justify the current market value of the property, has a special section known as "The Rent survey," which identifies similar rental charges in the neighborhood and compares them with the amount you charge for rent in the property you wish to buy.

The appraiser will interview other owners and tenants of similar properties in the neighborhood to investigate the amount of rent being paid and collected. This information should be readily available, as most building codes in various communities allow for multi-family units.

If there is a duplex in the area, there are likely several more of similar size and amenities. For example, suppose your new mortgage on your four-unit property is $3,000 per month, which includes principal and interest, taxes, and insurance.

You have three other tenants in the property who each pay $1,500 per month of rent to you. The lender will multiply the total amount of rent—in this case, $4,500—by .75 to arrive at the rental income used. How do you determine what rent to charge?

Your appraisal will tell you what the current market rent is for that area, and you should use this information when considering the amount to charge your tenants.

Tenants may have signed prior leases at a time when rent was lower than what the current market value is. For example, suppose you have three tenants and two pay $1,500 per month while one only pays $1,200 per month, according to their respective rental agreements.

When it is time for a renewal of the rental agreements, you must decide the amount to charge each one. If you find that the amount you charge per tenant is lower than other rental charges in your area, then it might be time to increase the rent in the renewal of your rental agreements.

You may also charge more for your units if your property is newer, updated, or remodeled. Essentially, you must ensure your cash flow is on the plus side and that you are not making any net losses.

Being a Landlord

In addition to making the commitment of buying a multi-family unit or keeping an existing home and renting it out, you must first decide if you wish to be a landlord at all.

Do you recall when you rented your first apartment? What happened when a problem arose, like a malfunction in the garbage disposal? What happened when a leak started in the kitchen sink or worse—when a toilet backed up, clogged and toilet water spilled onto the bathroom floor? What did you do then? You called your landlord or management immediately to fix these problems. The same thing will happen to you—your tenants will call you for issues that may arise.

When something goes wrong in one of your units—and it will—you can expect to be called upon at all hours to come and fix the problem. After all, the property is yours, not your tenant's. The best way to ensure that your property is stress-free is to ensure you have good tenants who don't stress you out. Good tenants pay on time and take care of your property. They're pleasant and don't call you constantly with trivial complaints. How do you find such tenants?

The best way is to treat well the tenants already occupying the property. If these tenants have paid you on time and taken care of the property, they are the tenants you will want to keep.

However, the property will be vacant at some point, and you'll need to evaluate your own rental applications when this is the case. You can find samples of lease agreements online or at office supply outlets, but the boilerplate is relatively simple.

There will be rules the tenants must follow regarding when rent is due, what the deposit amount is and how the deposit will be refunded when they move, along with a host of other requirements. Your tenants need to show proof of income and ability to pay rent on time.

In the same way mortgage lenders use debt ratios to qualify you for your own mortgage, you should also determine a prospective tenant's affordability prior to signing the lease.

Rental applications should indicate employment information such as the applicant's current employer, the amount of time they've been employed with said employer, and their monthly income. By having the applicants complete an authorization form allowing you to contact their employers directly, you can verify if the information contained within is accurate, as well as inquire on their employment history.

It is also advisable to contact the applicants' previous landlords and inquire on their payment patterns and history in taking care of the property. Moreover, unless you're a true handyman and can fix nearly anything, you'll want to assemble your own team of electricians, plumbers, and skilled workers whom you can call when you need help.

You may have worked with such professionals in the past. If you let each one know you're putting together your own rental management team, they may agree to discounted services if you use their services exclusively.

These people can also provide you with regular maintenance checks on the property, ensuring any needed maintenance and repairs are made before they become major expenses. Regular inspections and keeping the property in excellent shape are the best ways to avoid costly future repairs.

Finally, if you want to be an investor yet don't relish the idea of being a landlord, you can hire the services of a property management company. These firms are dedicated to helping property owners manage their rental units by acting on their behalf in such tasks as collecting monthly rent, inspecting and maintaining the property, and taking those dreaded midnight calls from tenants when there's a leak in the basement. Most property management firms will either require a portion of each tenant's monthly rent or a set fee; however, it is likely each can provide various services à la carte or full service.

Summary

- VA loans are used to finance primary residences only and cannot be used to purchase properties that will not be owner-occupied.

- When a veteran keeps a purchased house with a VA mortgage and buys another without using any remaining VA entitlement, the VA does not review the original VA mortgage retroactively.

- Borrowers can finance multiple properties, provided they qualify for both mortgages.

- Lenders can use rental income on properties in certain instances if the borrower has previous experience as a landlord.

- There are provisions that allow for the waiving of the landlord requirement, provided there is sufficient equity in the existing property and six months' worth of cash reserves for each property.

- Positive cash flow is essential for an investment property.

- Assemble a team of contractors that can help you with electrical, plumbing, and other maintenance issues.

- Prior to being a landlord, some factors require consideration as taking on the role will take additional effort. Property management companies exist to assist landlords with managing and maintaining rental properties.

16

HOLDING AND IMPROVING PROPERTY VALUE

When you own real estate, property value is important to you. As you build equity over the years, you want to protect it by ensuring the collateral—your property—is always at its peak.

Value is primarily determined by local real estate market conditions, but it is further enhanced by the state and appeal of the property itself.

Appearance

One of the most important ways to protect your investment and to continue building equity is the enhancement of your property's visual appeal. Your property makes its first impression to the outside world through its physical appearance, which serves as an indication that it is not simply a nice-looking property, but that it is a home with an updated exterior and that was clearly well cared for and properly maintained over the years.

This initial appearance is called "the curb appeal," and it is a description of your home from the street made by strangers passing by.

In your wish to enhance your house's curb appeal, the first thing to consider is a simple fresh coat of paint. It's also the most cost-effective improvement you can make. Hire a painting contractor to caulk and paint your home and make repairs as needed. If you're preparing to sell your home, then the color of your property—both inside and out—is an important consideration.

What color should you use? The most universal and generally appealing color is white. It's the cleanest of tones and the trim can be accented with any color of your choice.

A new coat of paint will highlight everything around it—including the roof. You may also want to closely inspect your roof, especially if it's been more than a few years since the shingles were replaced.

Maintaining an impeccable landscape that is clear of clutter is an important part of a home's curb appeal. Ensure your lawn is kept at a proper height and that shrubbery is well-trimmed. If you have a sidewalk and driveway, it's best to clean both thoroughly with a power washer, which will then give the concrete a fresh, new appearance.

Interior colors can be primarily earth tones, but your real estate agent will help you determine if your home needs a painting job. Not only is interior paint the most cost-effective way to freshen up your home, choosing the right colors can provide a warm, cozy atmosphere or brighten a smaller room with a lighter shade.

Upgrades

What do buyers seek when they're shopping for a home? Certainly, the most popular feature of a home is a large, updated kitchen with upgraded countertops and plenty of custom cabinet space.

Sparkling new appliances and clean food preparation areas will immediately add value to your home. Remodeling a kitchen can provide a greater return on an investment than any other upgrade.

Another "must have" feature for home buyers is a space that can be used as a study, or a home office where one can work from home, telecommute or simply conduct research on the internet.

New flooring can also be considered, especially if the floors are carpeted and show signs of wear. You can either have your carpets professionally cleaned or your real estate agent will ask that you replace the carpet with new flooring altogether. Wood floors are more expensive than carpet but provide a richer, more elegant feel.

In addition, master baths are also an asset for any home, especially when they provide luxuries such as separate sinks, shower and bath arrangements.

Sometimes, some simple new hardware that replaces old faucets and handles can provide a fresher, shinier look. Crown molding will also provide a finished look to any room and is a relatively inexpensive improvement.

When preparing to sell, your agent will help you get your home ready and may also suggest home staging, which involves an interior designer who redesigns your home's interior temporarily to make it even more appealing.

Home stagers have their own furniture and accessories they use, or work with your own possessions.

There is no end to the possibilities of upgrades; however, if you want the greatest return for your money, you can start by renovating your bathroom and kitchen, as well as painting the interior and exterior of your home. Avoid adding skylights, pools, whirlpools or hot tubs and fencing, as these are the worst returns on investment.

Finally, keep your home in top shape by paying for an inspection report.

An inspector will evaluate your current home from roof to basement, and everything in between. The inspector will look for signs of decay or water intrusion. They will walk on the roof and crawl in the attic. By having a thorough inspection performed every few years, you will be alerted to any potential problems that could occur in the future. If property owners do not have their homes regularly inspected or maintained, they will ultimately have thousands of dollars of needless repairs in their hands down the road. A well-maintained home is a savings account. It's an asset that builds equity over time. Taking care of your property will help your account grow faster. Plus, you'll have the nicest house on the block!

Summary

- Your home's appearance and level of maintenance helps protect your equity, which results in a higher sales price if or when you decide to sell.

- "Curb appeal" refers to the appearance of your home in the eyes of passersby as they view your home from the street.

- Exterior paint, immaculate lawns and clean walkways create positive curb appeal.

- Upgrades in baths and kitchens are the most appealing features of a property to potential buyers and they provide the greatest return on investment

- Homes offices and studies are a recent desired upgrade for home buyers.

- Painting is also another big return on investment and provides a fresh look to a home.

- Home stagers can be hired to present your home as most appealing to potential buyers.

- Regular home inspections by a professional inspector can help identify any necessary repairs or maintenance, which will ultimately help you avoid costly repairs in the future.

17

THE TRUE BENEFITS
OF HOMEOWNERSHIP

This book has tackled every aspect of financing a home with a VA loan, from the history of its inception, to loan types to income tax considerations and everything else in between.

We discussed at length the advantages of having a mortgage interest deduction during tax season, instead of sending rent checks to a landlord. We saw how property tax deductions can contribute to lower income taxes when they are deducted from taxable income and thus place borrowers in lower tax brackets.

We reviewed the various loan terms available and discovered how to keep monthly payments as low as possible while simultaneously keeping the amount of interest paid to the lender at lower levels through consideration of a 20- or 25-year fixed rate mortgage.

Key points were highlighted and explained when a refinance loan would be a good idea. We also covered how to calculate a recovery period. Closing costs are a part of all mortgage loans –VA loans included—and we discussed how to save money while using them and how to reduce necessary documentation by finding a good real estate agent.

Down payment requirements on certain loans and how to calculate them were reviewed, as well as the necessary steps to restore previously unused entitlement. Equity is built both through natural appreciation of property values and loan amortization, which gradually reduces the outstanding loan balance.

The combination of property appreciation and principal down payment rapidly increases the net worth of the homeowner. Long-term home ownership is consistently considered the single most effective way for consumers to build wealth.

This book explained the definitions and use of interest, amortization, escrows and impounds, insurance, restricted fees, debt ratios, hybrids, payments, principal, entitlements, loan guarantees and many more. You now have an inside knowledge of how VA loans work that few others possess.

However, we have not covered the true benefits of home ownership in any of the previous chapters. While there are many financial factors that require a homebuyer's consideration, we haven't discussed the pride that comes with home ownership.

Owning a property in the United States is a privilege found nowhere else in the world. Property rights are sacred, and if you comply with local regulations and zoning laws and pay your mortgage on time, you can do whatever you want with your property.

Home ownership is referred to by many as "The American Dream." This dream ultimately ties back to the freedom and liberties we have as citizens living in our great nation. As Americans, our opportunities and liberties are peerless.

Those who have been overseas can relate to this statement personally, as they have likely seen firsthand the daily obstacles encountered by citizens in other countries. Home ownership is one of the many privileges we have as Americans, and it is part of the way of life we have chosen to defend through our service.

In the end, the true benefit of owning a home is not about income tax benefits you'll receive as a homeowner, although there is a variety of those. Its true benefit is the feeling you get from knowing that when you lay down your head to sleep at night, you're sleeping in a home that belongs to *you*, and nobody else.

GLOSSARY

Abstract of Title - A written record of the property's historical ownership that helps to determine if transfer from one party to another is possible without any previous claims. An abstract of title is used in certain parts of the country to determine if there are any previous claims on the property in question.

Acceleration - A loan accelerates when it is paid off early, usually at the request or demand of the lender. An acceleration clause within a loan document states what must occur when a loan must be paid immediately. It usually applies to nonpayment, late payments, or the transfer of the property **without the lender's permission.**

Adjustable Rate Mortgage - A loan program where the interest rate may change throughout the life of the loan. An ARM adjusts based on agreed-upon terms between the lender and the borrower. However, it may typically only change once or twice a year.

Alternate Credit - Items you must pay each month but that won't appear on your credit report, such as your telephone bill. While such items aren't reported as installment or revolving credit, in relation to mortgage loans, they can establish your ability and willingness to responsibly make consistent payments. It is sometimes called "nonstandard credit."

Amortization - The length of time it takes for a loan to be paid off fully, by predetermined agreement. These payments are at regular intervals. It is sometimes called a "fully amortized loan." Amortization terms can vary, but generally accepted terms run in five-year increments, from ten to forty years.

Annual Percentage Rate - The cost of money borrowed, expressed as an annual rate. The APR is a useful consumer tool to compare different lenders; however, it is often not used correctly. The APR can only work when comparing the same exact loan type from one lender to another.

Appraisable Asset - Any item whose value can be determined by a third-party expert. For instance, that car you wish to sell is an appraisable asset. If the item can be appraised, then those funds can be used to buy a house.

Appraisal - A report that helps to determine the market value of a property. An appraisal can be done in various ways as required by a lender. This can range from their simply driving by the property to their ordering a full-blown inspection, complete with photographs. Appraisals compare similar homes in the area to substantiate the value of the property in question.

Appraisal Management Company - An independent third-party who receives appraisal orders from lenders or mortgage brokers, places the appraisal order and manages the appraisal ordering and receiving process.

APR - *See* Annual Percentage Rate.

ARM - *See* Adjustable Rate Mortgage.

Assumable Mortgage - Homes sold with assumable mortgages allow buyers to take over the terms of the loan, along with the house being sold. Assumable loans may be fully or non-qualifying assumable; in other words, buyers can take over the loan without being qualified or otherwise evaluated by the original lender. Qualifying assumable loans refer to loans wherein buyers may assume terms of the existing note; however, they must first qualify all over again as though they were applying for a brand-new loan.

Automated Valuation Model - An electronic method of evaluating a property's appraised value. This is achieved by scanning public records for recent home sales and other data in the property's neighborhood. Although not yet widely accepted as a replacement for full-blown appraisals, many in the industry expect AVMs to eventually replace traditional appraisals altogether.

AVM - *See* Automated Valuation Model.

Balloon Mortgage - A type of mortgage where the remaining balance must be paid in full at the end of a preset term. A five-year balloon mortgage might be amortized over a 30-year period, but the remaining balance is due in full at the end of five years.

Bridge Loan - A short-term loan primarily used to pull equity out of one property for a down payment on another. This loan is paid off when the original property sells. Since they are short-term loans, sometimes lasting just a few weeks, it is likely that only retail banks offer them. The borrower doesn't typically make any monthly payments, as they only pay off the loan when the property sells.

Buydown - Paying more money to get a lower interest rate is called a *permanent* buydown, and it is used in conjunction with discount points. The more discount points the buyer has, the lower their rate will be. A *temporary* buydown is a fixed rate mortgage that starts at a reduced rate for the first period, and then gradually increases to its final note rate. A temporary buydown for two years is called a "2-1 buydown." For a three- year buydown, it is referred to as a "3-2-1 buydown."

Cash-Out - A refinance mortgage involving the withdrawal of equity out of a home in the form of cash during a refinance. Instead of only reducing your interest rate during a refinance as well as financing your closing costs, you also finance even more as you can put the additional money in your pocket.

Closer - The person who helps prepare the lender's closing documents. The closer, or closing agent, forwards those documents to your settlement agent's office, where you will be signing your closing papers. In other states, a closer can also be the person who holds your loan closing.

Closing Costs - The various fees involved when buying a home or obtaining a mortgage. The fees, which are required to issue a good loan, can come directly from the lender or may come from others during the transactions.

Collateral - A property owned by the borrower that's pledged to the lender as security in the event the loan goes bad. A lender provides the borrower with a mortgage while using the borrower's house as collateral.

Comparable Sales - The section of an appraisal report that lists recent transfers of similar properties in the immediate vicinity of the house being bought. It is also referred to as "comps."

Conforming Loan - A conventional conforming loan, or a Fannie Mae or Freddie Mac loan, which is equal to or less than the maximum allowable loan limits established by Fannie and Freddie. These limits are changed annually.

Conventional Loan - A loan mortgage that uses guidelines established by Fannie Mae or Freddie Mac and that is issued and guaranteed by lenders.

Credit Report - A report that shows the payment histories of a consumer, along with the individual's property addresses and public records.

Credit Repository - A database where credit histories are stored. Merchants and banks agree to store the credit patterns of consumers in a central location that is accessible to other merchants and banks.

Credit Score - A number derived from a consumer's credit history and based on various credit details from a consumer's past and their likelihood of default. Credit patterns are assigned as specific numbers, and different credit activity may have a greater or lesser impact on the score.

The higher the credit score is, the better the consumer's credit becomes.

Debt Consolidation - Paying off all or part of one's consumer debt with home equity. Debit consolidation can be part of a refinanced mortgage or a separate equity loan.

Debt Ratio - The ratio that represents gross monthly payments divided by gross monthly income, expressed as a percentage. There are typically two debt ratios to consider, "The Housing Ratio" and "The Total Debt Ratio." The housing ratio, sometimes referred to as the "front-end" or "front ratio," is the total monthly house payment plus any monthly tax, insurance, private mortgage insurance, or homeowner's association dues, divided by gross monthly income. The total debt ratio, also referred to as the "back-end" or "back ratio," is the total housing payment plus other monthly consumer installment or revolving debt, also expressed as a percentage. Loan debt ratio guidelines are usually noted as 32/38, with 32 being the front ratio and the 38 being the back ratio. Ratio guidelines can vary from loan to loan and lender to lender.

Deed - A written document showing every ownership transfer of a property.

Deed in Lieu - An abbreviated term for "Deed in Lieu of a Foreclosure." A deed in lieu is completed by the borrower who transfers all interest in the property to the lender.

Deed of Trust - A written document provided as security to a third party, usually a lender, that indicates an interest in the home being bought.

Delinquent - The state of being behind on a mortgage payment. Payments that are late over 30-day increments are typically known as "30+ days delinquent," "60+ days delinquent," and "90+ days delinquent."

Discount Points - Also called "points," they are represented as a percentage of a loan amount. One point equals to 1% of a loan balance. Borrowers pay discount points to reduce the interest rate for a mortgage. Typically, each discount point paid reduces the interest rate by ¼ percent. It is a form of prepaid interest to a lender.

Document Stamp - A proof of evidence indicating the amount of tax paid upon transfer of ownership of property. It is usually validated with an ink stamp. Certain states call it by its shortened version, "doc stamp." Doc stamp tax rates can vary based on locale, and it is important to note that not all states have doc stamps.

Down Payment - The amount of money initially provided by the borrower to close a mortgage. The down payment equals the sales price, minus financing. It's the first amount of equity a homeowner will have from their new home.

Easement - A right of way previously established by a third party. Easement types can vary but they typically involve the right of a public utility to cross your land to access an electrical line.

Equity - The difference between the appraised value of a home and any outstanding loans recorded against the house.

Escrow - Depending on where the homeowner lives, an escrow can mean two different things. On the West Coast, for example, when a home goes under contract, it "goes into escrow" (*see also* Escrow Agent). In other parts of the country, an escrow is a financial account set up by a lender to collect monthly installments for annual tax bills and/or hazard insurance policy renewals.

Escrow Account - *See* Impound Account.

Escrow Agent - On the West Coast, the escrow agent is the person or company that handles the home closing, and who ensures documents are assigned correctly and that property transfer has been completed.

FACTA - *See* Fair and Accurate Credit Transactions Act.

Fair and Accurate Credit Transactions Act - The FACTA is new law that replaces the Fair Credit Reporting Act (FCRA) and governs the ways in which consumer information can be stored, shared, and monitored for privacy and accuracy.

Fair Credit Reporting Act - The FCRA was the first consumer law that emphasized consumer rights and protections relating to credit reports, credit applications, and privacy concerns.

Fannie Mae - *See* Federal National Mortgage Association.

FCRA - *See* Fair Credit Reporting Act.

Federal Home Loan Mortgage Corporation - The FHLMC, or more commonly known as "Freddie Mac," is a corporation established by the U.S. government in 1968 to buy mortgages from lenders made under Freddie Mac guidelines and is owned by the Federal Government.

Federal Housing Administration - Formed in 1934, the FHA is now a division of the Federal Housing Finance Agency (FHFA). It provides loan guarantees to lenders who make loans under FHA guidelines.

Federal Housing Finance Agency (FHFA) - Established as the result of the Housing and Economic Recovery Act of 2008, this agency controls Fannie Mae, Freddie Mac, HUD and the Federal Home Loan Banks.

Federal National Mortgage Association - The FNMA, or more commonly known as "Fannie Mae," was originally established in 1938 by the U.S. government to buy FHA mortgages and provide liquidity in the mortgage marketplace. It functions similarly to Freddie Mac. In 1968, its charter was changed and it now purchases conventional as well as government mortgages.

Federal Reserve Board - The head of the Federal Reverse Banks that sets overnight lending rates for banking institutions, among other things. Commonly known as "Fed," it does not set mortgage rates.

Fed Funds Rate - The rate banks charge one another to borrow money overnight.

Fed - Shorthand name for the Federal Reserve Board.

FHA - *See* Federal Housing Administration.

FICO - The acronym for Fair Isaac Corporation, the company that invented the most widely used credit scoring system.

Final Inspection - The last inspection of a property, showing that the newly built home is 100% complete or that a home improvement is 100% complete. It lets lenders know that their collateral and their loan are exactly where they should be.

Fixed Rate Mortgage - A loan whose interest rate does not change throughout the term of the loan.

Flood Certificate - A certificate that shows whether a property or part of a property lies above or below any local flood zones. These flood zones are mapped over the course of several years by the Federal Emergency Management Agency (FEMA). The certificate identifies the property's exact legal location and a flood line's elevation. It features a box with the simple question, "Is the property in a flood zone? Yes or No?" If the property is in a flood zone, the lender will require special flood insurance that is not usually carried under a standard homeowner's hazard insurance policy.

Foreclosure - A foreclosure occurs when the mortgage isn't repaid. Lenders begin the process of forcefully recovering their collateral when borrowers fail to make loan payments. The lender takes away the borrower's house .

Freddie Mac - *See* Federal Home Loan Mortgage Corporation.

Gift - When the down payment and closing costs for a home are given to the borrower rather than the funds coming from their own accounts, it is called a gift. Usually, such gifts only come from family members or established foundations that help new homeowners.

Gift Affidavit - A form signed whereby someone swears that the money they're giving to another person is indeed a gift and not a loan. It is used primarily for the purchase of a home. Lenders require proof of that completed form, as well as a paper trail of the gift funds added to the recipient's own funds.

Gift Funds - Monies given to a borrower for the sole purpose of buying a home. These funds are not to be paid back in any form and are usually given by a family member or a qualified nonprofit organization.

Government National Mortgage Association - The GNMA, or more commonly known as "Ginnie Mae," is a U.S. government corporation formed to purchase government loans like VA and FHA loans from banks and mortgage lenders.

Good Faith Estimate - A list of estimated closing costs on a specific mortgage transaction. This estimate must be provided to the loan applicants within 72 hours after receipt of a mortgage application by the lender or broker, or immediately if the application is given in person.

Hazard Insurance - A specific type of insurance that covers against certain destructive elements such as fire, wind, and hail. It is usually an addition to homeowner's insurance; however, every home loan has a hazard rider.

HELOC - *See* Home Equity Line of Credit.

Home Equity Line of Credit - HELOC is a credit line using a home as collateral. Customers write checks on this line of credit whenever they need to and pay only on balances withdrawn. It is much like a credit card, with the difference that it is secured by the property.

Homeowner's Insurance - An insurance policy that covers not only damage to the house due to catastrophic events or accidents, but also other things, such as liability or personal property.

Home Valuation Code of Conduct (HVCC) - A national lending rule which prohibits lenders or mortgage brokers from influencing property values by communicating directly with an appraiser. It provides rules for ordering, compensating and selecting an appraiser.

Impound Account - An account that is set up by a lender to deposit a monthly portion of annual property taxes or hazard insurance. As taxes or insurance come up for renewal, the lender pays the bill using these funds. It is also called an *escrow account.*

Inspection - A structural review of the house to determine defects in workmanship, damage to the property, or required maintenance. An inspection does not determine the value of the property. For example, a pest inspection inspects for termites or wood ants—not property value.

Installment Account - Borrowing one lump sum and agreeing to pay back a certain amount each month until the loan is paid off. A car loan is an example of an installment loan.

Interest Rate - The amount charged to borrowed money over a specified period.

Interest Rate Reduction Loan - An IRRL is a VA refinance loan program that has relaxed credit guidelines. It is also called a "streamline refinance."

IRRL - *See* Interest Rate Reduction Loan.

Jumbo Loan - A mortgage that exceeds current conforming loan limits.

Junior Lien - A second mortgage or one that subordinates to another loan. It is no longer as common term as it once was. The terms *second mortgage* or *piggyback* have superseded this outdated term.

Land Contract - An arrangement where the buyer makes monthly payments to the seller, but the ownership of the property does not change until the loan is paid in full.

Land-to-Value - An appraisal term that calculates the value of the land as a percentage of the total value of the home. If the land exceeds the value of the home, it's more difficult to find financing without good comparable sales. It is also called "lot-to-value."

Lease-Purchase Agreement - Also known as "rent-to-own." This refers to an option whereby a buyer leases a home until they have saved up enough money for down payment to qualify for a conventional mortgage.

Lender Policy - A title insurance that protects a mortgage from defects or previous claims of ownership.

Liability - An obligation or bill on the part of the borrower. It works like an automobile loan. When you pay off the car, you get the title. Liabilities such as student loans or a car payment can show up on a credit report, but they can also be anything else which you are obligated to pay. Such liabilities on the credit report are used to determine debt ratios.

Lien - A legal claim or prior interest on the property a buyer wishes to purchase. When someone borrows money from another source with the goal of buying a house, this could mean that they have a lien on that property.

Loan - Money granted to one party with the expectation of it being repaid.

Loan Officer - The person who is responsible for helping mortgage applicants get qualified and who assists in loan selection and application. Loan officers can work at banks, credit unions, and mortgage brokerage houses or for bankers.

Loan Processor - The person who gathers the required documentation for a loan application for submission. Along with your loan officer, a potential homebuyer works with the loan processor extensively during the mortgage process.

Loan Underwriter - The person responsible for ultimately approving or denying a loan application. The underwriter compares loan guidelines with what is have documented in the borrower's file.

Loan-to-Value Ratio - LTV is expressed as a percentage of the loan amount compared to the value of the home, which is determined by an appraisal. If a home was appraised at $100,000 and the loan amount was 70,000, then the LTV would be 70%.

LTV - *See* Loan-to-Value Ratio.

Market Value - In an open market, the market value of a property is both the highest the borrower is willing to pay and the least the seller is willing to accept at the time of contract. Property appraisals can justify the market value by comparing similar home sales in that property's neighborhood.

Mortgage - A loan with the property being pledged as collateral. The mortgage is retired when the loan is paid in full.

Mortgage Brokers - Companies that set up a home loan between a banker and a borrower. Brokers don't have money to lend directly, but they have experience in finding various loan programs that can suit the borrower, much like the way in which an independent insurance agent operates. Brokers don't work for the borrower; instead, they provide mortgage loan choices from other mortgage lenders.

Mortgagee - The person or business making the loan; also called the "lender."

Mortgagor - The person(s) getting the loan; also called the "borrower."

Multiple Listing Service - MLS is a central repository where real estate brokers and agents show homes and seek homes for sale.

Nonconforming - Loans whose amounts are above current Fannie or Freddie limits. *See also* Jumbo Loan.

Note - A promise to repay. It may or may not have property involved, and may or may not be a mortgage.

Note Modification - A process where a mortgage lender modifies the current structure of the outstanding note, often to assist a borrower who may be having difficulty making their regular mortgage payment as reflected by the original note.

Notice of Default (NOD) - Delivered by Certified Letter from the mortgage lender to the borrower when two successive mortgage payments have been missed. Because it is a legal process filing, the NOD becomes a public record and is stored in the county or parish where the property is located.

Origination Fee - A fee charged to cover costs associated with finding, documenting, and preparing a mortgage application. It is usually expressed as a percentage of the loan amount.

Owner's Policy - Title insurance made for the benefit of the homeowner.

Payment Shock - A term used by lenders which refers to the percentage difference between what the homebuyer is currently paying for housing and what their new payment will be. Most loan programs don't have a payment shock provision; however, for those that do, the common percentage increase is 150%.

PITI - An acronym for "Principal, Interest, Taxes, and Insurance." These figures help determine front debt ratios. In condos, townhouses or co-ops, Home Owner's Association dues replace the payment for insurance.

Portfolio Loan - A loan made by a direct lender, usually a bank. It is kept in the lender's loan portfolio instead of being sold or underwritten to any external guidelines.

Pre-foreclosure - A state of a property wherein foreclosure is imminent. It is often associated with an impending or current "Notice of Default," or NOD.

Prepaid Interest - TeDaily interest collected from the day of loan closing to the first of the following month.

Principal - The outstanding amount owed on a loan, excluding any interest that is due.

Quit Claim - A release of any interest in a property from one party to another. A quit claim does not, however, release the obligation on the mortgage.

Rate-and-Term Refinance - A type of refinancing that allows a new rate change. In this instance, the homebuyer is changing the interest rate and changing the term or length of the new note. This process requires a full approval process exactly as the purchase loan was issued.

Realtor - A member of the National Association of REALTORS and a registered trademark. However, not all real estate agents are realtors.

Recast - A term applied to ARMs and used when extra payments are made to the principal balance. When a homebuyer's note is recast, their monthly payment is calculated for them.

Refinance - Obtaining a new mortgage to replace an existing one. There is also a "rate-and-term refinance," where only the outstanding principal balance, interest due, and closing costs are included in the loan.

Reissue - When refinancing, there may be discounts if the borrower uses the same title agency. This "reissue" of an original title report can cost much less than a full title insurance policy.

Rescission - Withdrawal from a mortgage agreement. Refinanced mortgage loans for a primary residence have a required three-day "cooling off" period before the loan becomes official. If, for any reason, the borrower decides to no longer take the mortgage, they can "rescind" and cancel the request.

Reserves - A borrower's assets after closing. Reserves can include cash in the bank, stocks, mutual funds, retirement accounts, IRAs, and 401(k) accounts.

Revolving Account - A credit card or department store account on which the cardholder typically has a limit and doesn't make any payments until they charge something.

Sales Contract - Your written agreement to sell or purchase a home, which is signed by both the seller and buyer.

Second Mortgage - This is sometimes called a "piggyback" mortgage. It refers to a second mortgage that assumes a subordinate position behind the first mortgage. If the home goes into foreclosure, the first mortgage would be settled before the second could lay claim. *See also* Junior Lien.

Seller - The person transferring ownership and all rights for the current homeowner's property in exchange for cash or trade.

Settlement Statement - Also called the Final HUD-1. It shows all financial entries during the home sale, including sales price, closing costs, loan amounts, and property taxes. A borrower's initial good faith estimate will be their first glimpse of their settlement statement. This statement is one of the final documents put together before they can proceed with closing and it is prepared by their attorney or settlement agent.

Short Sale - When a property changes ownership from seller to buyer, the lender has agreed to accept less for their outstanding mortgage note than the current balance or payoff amount. The seller is then released from all future obligation to repay the mortgage and any delinquent amounts.

Survey - A map that shows the physical location of the structure of the house and where it sits on the property. A survey also designates any easements that run across or through the property.

Title Insurance - Protection for the lender, the seller, and/or the borrower against any defects or previous claims to the property being transferred or sold.

Title - Legal ownership of a property.

Title Exam/Title Search - The process wherein public records are reviewed to research any previous liens on the property.

Underwater Mortgage - A term used to describe a piece of leveraged real estate, where the mortgage balance exceeds the current property value.

VA Loan - A government mortgage guaranteed by the Department of Veterans Affairs.

VA No-No - A type of VA loan where the borrower not only puts *no* money down, but also pays *no* closing costs.

Verification of Deposit - A VOD is a form mailed to a bank or credit union that asks the institution to verify that the existence of a borrower's bank account, the amount of money in it, how long the borrower has had it, and what the average balance was over the previous two months.

VOD - *See* Verification of Deposit.

Wraparound Mortgage - A method of financing where the borrower pays the former owner of the property each month in the form of a mortgage payment. The former owner will then make a mortgage payment to the original mortgage holder. This method is not permitted without initial lender's permission.